TONGUE IN CHEEK

PHOTO CREDIT: CHRISTOPHER FRANCIS

Khyrunnisa A. is the author of the popular fortnightly column, 'Inside View', that appeared in *The Hindu MetroPlus*. She is also a prize-winning author of children's fiction and the creator of the hugely popular Butterfingers series for young readers.

She is a full-time writer and lives in Thiruvananthapuram.

Visit her at www.khyrunnisa.com and write to her at khyrubutter@gmail.com.

TONGUE IN CHEEK
THE FUNNY SIDE OF LIFE

Khyrunnisa A.

First published by Tranquebar, an imprint of Westland Publications Private Limited, in 2019

Published by Tranquebar, an imprint of Westland Books, a division of Nasadiya Technologies Private Limited, in 2022

No. 269/2B, First Floor, 'Irai Arul', Vimalraj Street, Nethaji Nagar, Allappakkam Main Road, Maduravoyal, Chennai 600095

Westland and the Westland logo, Tranquebar and the Tranquebar logo are the trademarks of Nasadiya Technologies Private Limited, or its affiliates.

Copyright © Khyrunnisa A., 2019

Khyrunnisa A. asserts the moral right to be identified as the author of this work.

ISBN: 9789395073318

10 9 8 7 6 5 4 3 2 1

The views and opinions expressed in this work are the author's own and the facts are as reported by her, and the publisher is in no way liable for the same.

All rights reserved

Typeset by Jojy Philip, New Delhi 110015
Printed at Nutech Print Services - India

No part of this book may be reproduced, or stored in a retrieval system, or transmitted in any form or by any means, electronic, mechanical, photocopying, recording, or otherwise, without express written permission of the publisher.

For my husband, Vijaya Kumar, who strayed into the book and stayed there

Contents

Author's Note   xi

GASTRONOMICAL GLITCHES

Kulchas, Phulkas, Snakes and Chaps	3
Where's the Rubber Band Gone?	6
The Trouble with Eggs	9
Packed with Adventure	12

WEDDING WOWS

The Gold Rush	17
Food for Thought	20
Parking Worries	23
The Case of the Lost Key	26

JUST WHAT THE DOCTOR ORDERED

Nerves of Steel	31
Half a Worm is Better than None	34
Gym Eves	37
The New Smoking	40
The Appeal of Vegetable Peels	43

DIY Misadventures

A Tyre-ing Job	49
Losing Sleep over Waste	52
The Gentle Art of Washing Up	55
Rule of Thumb	58

Tech Age Hitches

Planet of the Apps	63
Picture Imperfect	66
The Aahs and the Ouches of the Computer Age	69

Fun in the City

Meetings	75
Getting Inked	78
Gated Community	81
Cats, Rats and Mangoes	84

Kitchen Blips

Under Pressure	89
The Cool Saviour	92
The Microwave Rules	95
The Gas Man Cometh	98

Of Creatures Great and Small

It's a Dog's Life, Anyway	103
Gazing at Fish	106
Cat-astrophe	109
Termite Alert!	112

On the Move

A Pony Ride	117
Hips or Chips?	120
Chasing the Parcel	123
'Booking' a Seat	126
No Directions, Please	129

Home Affairs

Not Floored	135
The Summer of Heat	138
Fresh as Paint	141
The Elusive Newspaper	144

Misadventures in the Garden

A Snake is a ... Snake	149
Coconut Shy	152
Orchids are Forever	155

Shopping Woes

Skin Deep	161
Nothing is Free	164
Atishoo, Atishoo!	167

Whose Word is it Anyway?

Serving Great Britain	173
Bored Games	176
The She I Love	179
Aunty or Madam	182

Author's Note

BEFORE ALL ELSE, THE 'CLAIMER' (THE OPPOSITE OF A 'disclaimer,' in case the word had you stumped)—this is a work of non-fiction. Names, places and incidents are not entirely the product of the author's imagination and every resemblance to any actual person, living or dead, creature, great or small, events, momentous or trivial and locales, exotic or familiar, is deliberate.

It all happened to me. Yes, every single incident in the book—the sublime (please search hard for these) and the ridiculous—actually took place. I have used artistic licence to add more spice to the narration. Which writer doesn't? But a close reading of the book will convince you about the authenticity of the incidents. Of course, if you continue to be sceptical, ask my husband, the reluctant partner, uneasy accomplice, disgruntled associate, unwitting ally, absent-minded spouse and the yin to my yang in many of the misadventures. He is generally truthful but if he asserts that there is merely some tenuous connection to reality, please don't take his word for it. He is only getting his back on me for having dragged him into the pages of a newspaper supplement fortnight after fortnight.

I'm grateful that *The Hindu MetroPlus*, which first published my articles in the column 'Inside View', gave me the freedom to choose my topics as long as there was humour in them. So, I promptly put my husband in them. I then added family, friends, relatives, pets, pests, the environment and just about anything that made up my day-to-day life.

This had some unforeseen side effects. Some friends began to move away when they saw me approach, nervous they would find themselves in the articles. Others wished to be mentioned by name and were miffed I had merely referred to them as friends. A friend took strong exception to my calling him an acquaintance. 'I thought I was your friend. Acquaintance, am I?' he raged and unfriended himself.

There were topics all around waiting to be chronicled. I discovered, with rather extraordinary consequences, that the fridge isn't just a necessity but a store house of culinary relicts, and a pressure cooker doesn't merely cook; it sometimes exhibits unique skills and moves off the stove to perform an impressive dance. Heating food in the microwave could well result in the manufacture of military arsenal, having fish in a tank can lead to solving an unusual murder mystery and cutting vegetables for a salad could be a lesson in beauty treatment!

How can life be dull when harmless rubber bands conspire to convert themselves into missiles, dead rats get delivered at your gate with regularity, and the simple task of getting your house painted takes on the hues of a guerrilla ambush?

The people you meet in your daily life are no less extraordinary. Auto drivers are actually philosophers in disguise, neighbours stun you with their architectural expertise, waiters speak volumes through the language of silence and gas delivery men wear a cloak of invisibility.

I hope this book will be handy in alerting you to the pitfalls and mini disasters that are just around the corner. But if you still manage to encounter them, then my simple advice would be to grin and bear it.

Khyrunnisa A.

GASTRONOMICAL GLITCHES

Kulchas, Phulkas, Snakes and Chaps

NEVER SAY ONE THING WHILE MEANING ANOTHER WHEN YOU place an order in a restaurant. Or say it at your peril, as I found out the other day when my son Amar's friends took us out to dinner. Everyone turned to me for the main order and suddenly nervous about making the key gastronomical decision, I stammered, 'Kulchas', when I meant 'phulkas'.

Kulcha, for those unfamiliar with the dish, is leavened Indian flatbread made from maida or all-purpose flour. Excellent description, the 'all-purpose' flour, for when kneaded into dough, it takes on the qualities of rubber, gum and glue with the least amount of fuss. Phulka, which is very close in spirit and texture to roti, is the more modest but healthier cousin of kulcha. It is unleavened flatbread made from wheat flour and generally dry and light.

'How many?' asked the waiter. Blissfully unaware of my mistake and gaining in confidence, I said, 'Ten'. After all, in spite of other dishes ordered, I was sure the five of us could easily manage two fluffy phulkas each. 'Actually, make that twelve,' I corrected myself, ordering an extra couple for the more ravenous amongst us. After placing the order I felt the warm glow of satisfaction that comes from a job well done. The waiter raised his eyebrows at me and left.

After the mandatory wait of half an hour, a waiter started bringing in some of the dishes we had ordered. He was followed by the one who had taken our order. This man didn't come in as much as stagger in, his hands weighed down by the laden plates he was barely able to balance. He plonked them before me and I was aghast to find the large plates heaped with giant kulchas gleaming wickedly with oil. Being rather thick and big, they had been halved and that explained the two plates. Twenty-four halves, each the size of two parathas combined. 'But these are kulchas!' I protested, pushing back my chair in my agitation and almost falling off it. 'I ordered phulkas.'

'No, Madam, you ordered kulchas.'

I turned disbelievingly to the others. 'Did I?'

'You did,' three voices chorused. The fourth, that of my husband, was mute, for he had already begun tucking into the just-arrived noodles, oblivious to all else. Never one to experiment with food, he orders noodles on all occasions, unless it isn't on the menu.

Some time was lost in clarifications, precious time, as it turned out, for it helped the kulchas turn cold and limp. Anyone with past experience of kulcha, naan or the Kerala parota—relatives all—knows they have to be eaten hot. I gamely took one as did the others. It felt like leather and behaved like elastic as I tugged and pulled with all my strength. And it tasted like rubber. As I chewed dutifully and laboriously, my jaws ached. Throwing table manners to the winds, I used both hands to tear off another piece. Someone quickly ordered chapatis as a chunk of kulcha rocketed to the next table.

I appealed to Ajay, my son's friend. A strapping six-footer with a gargantuan appetite, he is the trencherman who generally does the mopping up. He felt sorry for me and took two more halves, but the others gave them a wide berth. I hate the idea of food being wasted; so I asked for the rest of the kulchas, eighteen halves in all, to be parcelled. And thus began my kulcha days—kulcha for breakfast, kulcha for lunch, kulcha for supper and kulcha in between. Three days later Ajay called to ask what was for dinner. I asked him to take three guesses. Prompt came the reply, 'Kulcha, kulcha, kulcha?' 'Yes, yes, yes,' I responded.

This was an error of my own making, but certain menu cards make delightful mistakes and offer you very diverting fare. I remember coming across 'sweat' cakes under the heading 'Evening Snakes' which made me very curious about morning snakes. Another hotel offered a range of guptas—vegetable gupta, paneer gupta, cauliflower gupta, among others. This foxed me for a while. Could these be special dishes prepared using recipes carefully preserved from the Golden Age of the Guptas? But no, they were actually koftas. Then there were mutton 'chaps' and finger 'chaps' on offer. This wasn't blatant cannibalism at work, it was only very harmless (not for the goat, though) mutton chops and finger chips. 'Gopi' Manchurian and alu 'gopis' dance enticingly on the menu. Sand 'witches' appear spellbinding, meatless chicken sounds like a riddle waiting to be cracked, while 'boreyani' doesn't tempt.

With eating out becoming so common, one should be on their guard especially while choosing from such creative menus. I learnt it the hard way. I'm off kulchas forever but my jaws still ache.

Where's the Rubber Band Gone?

I TUGGED AT THE RUBBER BAND TIED AROUND A PACKET OF coriander powder only to have it snap with a ping and zip off like a rocket to land I knew not where. This happened one morning when I was making potato curry, in a hurry, as usual. A rubber band breaking was nothing new, but on all previous occasions it had unerringly found the tip of my nose. My nose, being of less than modest proportions, may not be easy to locate, but the rubber band certainly is, when my face comes in its trajectory and it aborts its travel plans to land bang on the centre. My quick, protective reflex action helps me secure it.

But that day the rubber band took off adventurously in an unknown direction. Had it landed in the curry? I peered closely, then taking the biggest ladle I could find, stirred it carefully. I scooped out a ladleful and poured the curry slowly back into the pan, examining it like a hawk to spot anything that could be the remains of the band. Wait, was that it? I peered harder. No, it was an unusually long and fine piece of onion, cut in a rare moment of artistry and finesse. Another red herring in the form of a shrivelled chilly gave me some hope until I identified it. Would the rubber band have dissolved in the heat, I wondered.

Maybe it hadn't found its final destination in the curry after all. Buoyed up by this reflection I quickly went on all fours in the kitchen. That was how my husband found me when he came, seeking breakfast. 'Er...um... something's fallen, I'm looking for it,' I explained. He had guessed as much, he said, it not being my regular practice to navigate around the kitchen on all fours.

The maid breezed in late to find me crawling at my husband's feet. She was delighted to have arrived at an emotionally charged moment and her face fell when I jumped up to explain. Robbed of drama, she curtly said she would sweep the place carefully and together we guided the broom to hitherto uncharted territories. The exercise yielded two ancient cashew nuts that crumbled on contact, dry curry leaves, drier chillies, a rusty blade and a piece of foul smelling ginger but, alas, no rubber band.

I now decided on an experiment. Wrapping a rubber band tightly around a packet of masala powder, I tried to set it free, so I could observe the direction in which it would fly. It wouldn't even snap, the perverse thing, and remained stubbornly resilient, attaching itself to the packet like its long lost love. It is a truth universally acknowledged that if a rubber band has to break, it will, and conversely, if it doesn't wish to, it won't.

Another idea struck me. What goes up must come down, but what if the rubber band hadn't? I climbed on a high stool and simulating a dangerous ballet act, tried to examine the tops of the built-in cupboards. I found interesting carcasses of cockroaches and spiders in various stages of decomposition but the dust set me off on a sneezing spree and I abandoned the search.

At breakfast, my husband complimented me on the tasty curry. 'What did you put in it?'

'Er... only the usual. Sometimes when you cook under time constraints, the food turns out tastier,' I explained, guiltily pleased but still a little apprehensive. Had I serendipitously stumbled upon a delicious variation of the curry, seasoned with bits of rubber band? When I ate, I rolled every particle of the serving carefully in my mouth to see if I could chance upon the errant rubber loop. For the first time I ate as one is expected to eat, masticating slowly and not swallowing the food in a rush, as I normally do.

Later I asked my husband if consuming rubber is dangerous. He looked quizzical, then reminisced, 'Not likely. Remember our school days when kids who had parents in Malaysia or Singapore brought delicious looking, sweet smelling, translucent erasers to school? They looked so attractive, we would take tiny bites when the owners weren't looking and pass them around.'

As absurd as it sounded, I did remember. All who had tasted those bits of rubber have survived, probably their insides strengthened, toughened and stretched by the strange ingestion. The secret of their success. And I have also lived to tell my tale...

The Trouble with Eggs

I ALWAYS THOUGHT CARROTS WERE GOOD FOR YOUR EYES. SO I began to devour carrots at a rate that would have given rabbits a complex, if they only knew. I didn't care much for the taste, but munched gamely along, and was just beginning to develop a taste for the healthy veggies when there appeared this friend who announced it wasn't carrots that are good for your eyes but eggs. 'Eggs?' I was surprised.

'Eggzactly!' she grinned.

'The whole egg or just the white?' I asked. The egg, especially its yolk, is often the bête noire of health faddists.

'The egg, the whole egg and nothing but the egg,' she declared, her eyes shining behind her glasses. Clearly, the eggs hadn't begun working the magic on her eyes yet.

She added, 'I've been studying eggs.' I thought she was studying economics, but I let that pass. 'It's a complete meal,' the wannabe oologist concluded.

'Likely,' I thought, considering it goes on to become a full-grown chicken, and if a chicken isn't a complete meal, then what is? This satisfying inference already set my mouth watering. I no longer wished to chicken out of eating an egg. Still, I wanted further clarification. 'What about the cholesterol in the yolk?' I persisted. 'Health gurus have been shouting themselves hoarse about the villainous egg yolk for some time.'

'Well, the turncoats have changed their tune, like this,' she said, snapping her fingers to show how fickle they were. 'Yolk is the hero now. If you value your eyesight, go for eggs. Don't take a jaundiced view of the yellow. There is good cholesterol in egg yolk. Believe me, it will raise your HDL levels.'

Her words raised my hopes of a delicious meal anyway. I was only too willing to believe her, for I love eggs. Visions of a variety of egg preparations—bull's eye, sunny side up, scrambled, boiled, not to mention teased into a fluffy omelette—rose before my eyes. I decided to buy some eggs the same day.

But the problem with eggs is that they are fragile. They break easily. They haven't been taught manners, they crack without a warning. They don't know that self-respecting eggs ought not to cave in to outside force without fighting back. And they create so much extra work for the one who exerted that force, although inadvertently. I remember how, during my egg-devouring days, bringing eggs home without breaking any, was a cause for celebration. And celebration was always in the form of breaking an egg for an omelette.

So, when I actually bought and brought home half a dozen eggs intact that evening, I couldn't believe it. This was a feat nonpareil and elated, I plonked the bag, a little too firmly, on the hard kitchen counter. Plop! Crrrack! In one stroke, half the job of getting an omelette ready was done. Unfortunately, both the egg shell and the paper cone that contained the eggs were determined to become ingredients too—the broken egg shell pieces clung to the messy mix while the soggy paper cone that had once contained the eggs was loath to miss out on the action. I had no choice but to throw the bag away, eggs, paper, shell and all.

The next half hour was devoted to wiping the counter clean, the bag having sported a tear, but the greater challenge was to rid the place of the stink. All the perfumes of Arabia got their act together and once the smell of egg was replaced with that of a blend of antiseptic and liquid cleaner, I was back in the store for more eggs and some provisions.

Shopping done, I jumped into an auto, my hand resting protectively over the paper packet of eggs that nestled on top of my carry bag. I had rescued the eggs from the bottom where the store assistant had deemed fit to place it. Call it sadistic pleasure, ignorance or sheer carelessness, some assistants love to deposit delicate food items like bread, plantains and eggs right at the bottom. But after all the care I had taken, the auto lurched, the bag swayed, the eggs fell to the floor of the auto. My dismayed shout startled the driver who jammed the brakes so hard the packet tumbled out of the auto.

'Don't you want that?' asked the driver, turning to glance at the unidentifiable bundle on the road.

'No, go on straight ahead,' I said, happy I didn't have to clean the mess this time.

Once home, I took a carrot out of the fridge and began chomping on it.

Packed with Adventure

'WHAT WAS SPECIAL FOR BREAKFAST TODAY?' A FRIEND ASKED my husband on the evening of Thiruonam. Strange, asking about breakfast when Onam's all about lunch. But he probably believed in working his way to the most important meal. 'Dosas,' my husband replied. The friend looked disappointed. 'Just dosas? What about yesterday?' he asked, though there was really no need for that sort of cross-examination. 'Dosas,' was the response. 'And in case you're curious about tomorrow, it's dosas again.' 'Yet again, you mean,' the friend corrected, giving me that look I invariably receive when conversation runs along these lines. It's a look I've begun to dread, one that speaks volumes, the gist of the volumes being, 'What sort of a cook are you?'

Pushed to the defensive, I quickly offered an explanation. 'He says idlis make him hungry very quickly, puris are oily, appams are preferred for dinner, ditto with chapatis. So what does that leave?' I asked. 'Dosas,' the friend responded mechanically. 'But what do you have with it? I'm sure the variety comes in the accompaniment.'

'Er...well, if one day it's dosas and chutney, the next day it is chutney and dosas. The day after it is dosas and...'

'Chutney again?' the friend interrupted, getting into the spirit of the game. 'Yes, it is!' I assented, imitating the quiz master of BBC's *Brain of Britain*, a popular radio programme. 'A watery reincarnation of the previous day's.'

'The chutney's finally getting over?' The clever guy was spot on with another inspired guess.

'Right again. The fourth day it is stew and dosas and after that...'

'Dosas and stew,' he interrupted. 'That leaves two more days...'

'Dosas and sambar and finally sambar and dosas,' said everyone in an exultant chorus.

Now that breakfast was exhaustively done with, he progressed to lunch. 'How was the sadya? How many payasams and pachadis did you make?'

'Make? What do you mean, make?' I asked. 'We bought the food.'

'What? Sacrilege!' he exclaimed, giving me an intense version of that "you must be a hopeless cook" look. He doesn't know I'm actually a hopeful cook; I keep hoping my cooking gets better or the taste buds of those on whom I experiment get worse.

I rushed to explain again. Till last year, we made every item for Onam at home. By we, I mean my help who...er...helped me, and I. To be fair, it was the other way around; my help did most of the cooking while I helped by hanging around as official taster and getting in her way. But once she left, I found Onamsadya preparation too much to handle. I decided to follow the lead of many worthy citizens and order from an eatery.

I had to agree with the friend when he observed that food from a hotel wouldn't be a patch on home-made stuff. The previous day we had been invited to my friend Anuradha's house for lunch where everything, including the chips and the ada for the payasam had been lovingly and expertly made at home. The food had just melted in our mouths.

But the sadya from the restaurant came packed with adventure. For one, we weren't sure of the order in which each item was to be served on the leaf; we weren't even sure how to place the leaf. Heated discussions and a few phone calls later, we began the serving only to discover that what we had thought was mango pickle was actually ginger, while we served 'olan' as white lime pickle. The order was hastily abandoned.

In a true tragedy of errors, payasam was served as paruppu, and ghee was poured over it liberally, watery white payasam was taken to be buttermilk and the sambar looked so much like theeyal we thought a revolutionary change in the sadya curries had been effected. What seemed to be pachadi was actually a sweet curry the likes of which we had never tasted before and which we never wish to taste again.

To compound the challenges, someone sat on the packet of pappadams and we used spoons to serve it, powdered. The plantain had arrived squashed, which someone wisecracked was a good thing since it facilitated the blending of it into the brown payasam, which was actually a mixed vegetable dish in disguise. We found the packets of pachadis after lunch.

But eating together is great fun and I wouldn't trade the chatty, hilarious, suspense-filled lunch of that day for anything. 'If only Mahabali and the packaged food came more often!' I observed to the friend.

WEDDING WOWS

The Gold Rush

'DO PEOPLE IN KERALA BUY GOLD BY THE KILO?' ASKED A FRIEND from another state. She had come to attend a 'typical Kerala wedding' and her jaw had dropped as she watched the bride make her coy way to the decorated stage, bent to the shape of a comma by the weight of the ornaments on her person. When the bride came to a full stop at the centre of the stage and turned towards the wedding guests with a reverential dignity forced on her by her accoutrements, the friend exclaimed, 'Oh, wow, so much gold! Kerala must be really rich.'

'Of course,' I replied. 'Gold is the bride of Kerala, I mean the pride of Kerala. Didn't you notice the hoardings advertising jewellery showrooms on your way here? Some of the models might be from the north, but the customers are native. And if it isn't jewellery, it is silk sarees, spun with pure gold thread, that seem to swirl and billow tantalisingly out of billboards. Welcome to Kerala, gold's own country.'

Brevity used to be the soul of Kerala weddings. Where have they gone, the refreshingly short weddings of long ago when the ceremony got over almost as soon as it had begun and guests who missed the bus or were delayed by a sneezing fit, found themselves escorted, to their great delight, straight to the dining hall?

The other recommending feature of a Malayalee wedding was the simplicity of the protagonists of the function. The last half century has seen the shift from the unostentatious bride, clad in an elegant cream silk saree and wearing a few ornaments on her person to set off her beauty, to the gold-armoured avatar of today. Not to be found wanting, the groom too has undergone an image makeover. The trademark dhoti and the plain off-white shirt are now passé; he's in silk too—a garish silk kurta and a shiny expensive dhoti. He would have preferred a sherwani or churidar-kurta but for the practical difficulty of sitting cross-legged in such an attire. To complete the picture, he flaunts a beauty-parloured face and a haircut that bears the stamp of an expert hair stylist.

It's not just a ceremony anymore, it is an event, and event managers have stepped in to make it the greatest show on earth. They go overboard trying to outdo each other in innovativeness with the result that there are themed weddings, fusion weddings and weddings at expensive resorts or at unique locations. The guests receive an invitation that is more a glossy, professionally designed, multi-paged, stone-encrusted and scented brochure than a simple card. Each leaf takes you through the bewildering programmes planned and only some close reading reveals when the actual nuptials will take place.

Weddings of today, many of them preceded by an elaborate betrothal ceremony, have transmogrified into mega events spread over a few days. I remember the excellent, thought-provoking speech made by a former police officer, a non-Keralite, at a College Day function. He said it was truly unfortunate that Kerala, instead of setting an example to the rest of the country with its unfussy and short wedding ceremony, was borrowing liberally from the elaborate, showy functions of the northern states. 'Sangeet', 'mehendi' and 'haldi' ceremonies followed by extravagant receptions attended by the whole world have become part of the wedding festivities here. He exhorted the audience to show character and courage and take the lead in reversing the trend. The moustachioed gentleman-officer's speech was, unfortunately, not as warmly received as it should have been.

Alas, the nuptial ceremonies are only getting more lavish by the day. They present a classic case of conspicuous consumption. The ups and downs of the gold market have never impacted the purchasing power of people here. When I asked an acquaintance why she didn't put an end to this gold craze and needless display of wealth, she replied, 'But what will people say?'

'Who are these "people"?' I asked.

'Relatives, neighbours, friends, guests ...' she reeled off.

'Give them something to say,' I suggested. She was appalled. 'Can't. Our self-respect is at stake. Besides, my daughter wants this.'

Ah, there lies the catch. So much for the modern 'emancipated' woman. And the less said about the 'progressive' male who maintains a selective silence when plans for the wedding are made, the better.

Now I'm off to a wedding where the groom will be received by a caparisoned elephant, or is he going to arrive on an elephant? I'm not sure, but the lunch is bound to be delicious, all nine courses of it.

Food for Thought

'DO YOU KNOW THERE WERE ONLY EIGHTY INVITED GUESTS in all?' A friend who had attended a wedding in the UK was describing the experience. He was full of praise for the function and the party that followed, but appeared a little bewildered too. 'Only eighty, can you beat it, and that included the families of the bride and groom. A total of just eight tables with every guest allotted a particular seat.' After attending weddings here where half the population is invited and the other half gatecrashes, he had every right to sound astonished.

'Can you change seats?' I asked, intrigued. This sounded like booking tickets for a movie. 'No way,' he replied. 'You have to take the allotted seat. I can't imagine something like this happening in our part of the world.'

I can't, either. Kerala weddings have always been known for their brevity, but the austerity that used to be associated with them is gone. Everyone's invited to witness the extravaganza. The hall is huge, the decorations ostentatious—event management has seen to that—the bride is covered with gold, flowers and silk, in the order of visibility, while the groom looks self-conscious and uncomfortable in an 'Indian' costume. He need not be, for the guests have come with their priorities firmly in place. The bride, the groom and the ceremony are mere trappings; the feast is the thing.

The beating of the drums and the nadaswaram rising to a crescendo signal the tying of the thali around the bride's neck. It signals something else for the guests—time to make a dash for the dining hall. The most coveted seats in the wedding auditorium are those nearest the doors to the gastronomical heaven and many canny guests take strategic positions there, already half out of their seats in their eagerness to sprint at the right moment.

Before you know what's happening, almost all the guests rush out as if the fire alarm has been sounded. And then begins the jostling, pushing and shoving. The wedding feast is a great leveller. Class, caste and gender distinctions are ignored while good manners are thrown to the winds in this mad rush to sit reverentially before the banana leaf. The well-heeled rub silk-covered shoulders with the down-at-heel, men ungallantly push women aside while women, not to be outdone, return the compliment—all for the cause of equality, of course. Children cheerfully bring down old grandmothers, students think nothing of aiming well-directed elbows into whomever stands in their way and all seems to be fair in the love for food and the war to reach it. Those with the swiftest feet and the quickest reflexes manage to gain entry and the doors close, leaving high, dry and hungry, a huge group that is left rueing its lack of initiative.

These days it's not just feasting that is important, but telling the whole world you have feasted. The other day I noticed a young chap taking a picture on his phone of the leaf with food served on it. 'Whatever for?' I asked my husband. 'To put up on Facebook, what else?' he replied. One can imagine the 'likes' that would appear and the comments: 'Wow, three rows of curries! You lucky dude!' 'I'm hungry!', 'Oh for the taste of Kerala. Homesick!' 'What's that interesting looking item, middle row, third from right?'...

The hungry ones, watching hawk-eyed from behind the glass doors and windows, perk up the moment they see the buttermilk being served. 'Over!' they announce to their ravenous companions. Before the first group can exit, they rush in, causing a stampede of sorts, while the catering manager and the long-suffering uncle of the bride seek to bring some order into the proceedings, all in vain.

'Allow us to clear the tables first,' they plead, trying to close the doors but it is too late. 'So what if the used leaves are just being cleared? We aren't finicky or squeamish, are we?' the self-appointed spokesperson of the group asks rhetorically, as all scramble for seats and watch with satisfaction the leaves being taken away, fresh ones being placed and curries being served.

If you chance to glance at the stage as you leave with a satisfied burp, you might find the bride and groom in a corner looking lost, waiting patiently to be led to the dining hall.

Parking Worries

INVITATIONS TO WEDDINGS START TRICKLING IN ONCE the mating season, I mean the wedding season, sets in. And much as the prospect of giving them the miss is tempting, familial bonds and ties of friendship force you to participate in them.

My husband greets any reminder of a wedding to attend with a heartfelt groan that speaks volumes. I know he's already agonising over where to park the car. He's not being paranoid—parking is not easy even on a normal day, and when a big fat wedding is on, it is next to impossible.

I'm pretty clueless about driving and traffic rules, which makes me blissfully optimistic about finding parking space, much to his annoyance. But I still hold that this concern about where to park is a male thing. I've never heard women drivers complain about it. 'That's because they park just about anywhere,' my husband retorts. 'And get away with it too.' I don't respond to this gender biased remark; there is some truth in it.

The two-wheeler is therefore a more sensible option, but not when it rains, as it did last week. As we approached the venue by car, I helpfully pointed out possible parking spots, all of which were rejected outright. 'Not enough space.' My protest that our car was a small Maruti Alto and not a six door Benz or a trailer bus went deservedly unheeded. 'What about parallel parking?' I asked. I had picked up that phrase from him. A telling grunt. Undeterred, I made more suggestions and got the occasional terse response. 'Can't you see the "No Parking" sign?', 'That's a gate'...and finally an exasperated, 'That's a police station, for heaven's sake!' shut me up.

His normal practice is to drop me off at the venue and then proceed to park the car in one end of the world. He then walks back to the hall, half hoping he will miss the wedding. In the rare instance that we both emerge from the car together, he strides rapidly ahead, trying to sneak in a bit of his daily walk while I trot a few paces behind like the proverbial Indian wife.

This time he didn't stop at the venue, having miraculously spotted some free space in front of a heap of gravel near a construction site. He scrutinised the area minutely for any prohibitive signs and after ensuring we wouldn't obstruct even a cyclist or a pedestrian, he said, 'We'll risk it,' and parked the car at an awkward angle over the gravel.

Risk was the right word; for me that is, but I had no idea at the time. He got off, locked the car and walked nonchalantly away, quite sure I would follow. But I hadn't reckoned with the mountain of gravel on my side and found it very difficult to manoeuvre a way out. I could open the door just a teeny bit. A little more and the stones would scrape it. I cautiously opened the door, and with an acrobatic wriggle found my way out. Pleased with my successful exit I stood awkwardly balanced on one foot. Thus poised, I managed to push the lock in and banged the door shut only to find I had locked in a good length of my saree pallav too. No amount of tugging would release it.

So there I was, well and truly stuck to the car, locked in an odd embrace with it while to my left the gravel loomed like an intimidating giant. My husband was nowhere to be seen. Maybe I could give him a call? I peered inside the car, to see if he had taken his mobile and found he hadn't. I also spotted my purse resting on the floor.

I've heard that a hairpin can open a Maruti's door and was annoyed with myself for not having one handy right now. What now? The clouds were beginning to gather and it looked like it would rain any moment. And then I spotted him in the distance at the zebra crossing.

Throwing all sense of decorum to the winds, which were swishing and swirling about, I called his name aloud. He has always maintained that his name is one of the commonest—Tom, Dick and Vijayakumar, he would quip—and that day I found he wasn't wrong. Half the people on the road turned in answer to the shortened version, he included. Or maybe it was just the shock of hearing a loud unintelligible shriek. Whatever it may be, my purpose was served and I was freed.

Taking an auto is easily the safest option.

The Case of the Lost Key

'WHERE'S MY KEY? GONE!' MY HUSBAND HALTED IN HIS TRACKS in dismay, then performed some intricate dance steps, eyes searching the ground, right hand deep in his trouser pocket. We had been strolling towards the car park after attending a wedding, a heavy lunch inside us and a friend, whom we had brought along, walking beside us.

'Key? What key?' I asked.

'The car key!' he snapped. 'Did you think I was talking about the Treasury strong room's keys?' He calmed down and sheepishly confessed, 'There's a hole in my trouser pocket.'

'But I darned it the other day,' I protested. 'That was the other pocket,' he clarified. The hole in that pocket had been discovered when, trying hard to keep pace with him as he marched ahead, I almost stepped on his mobile phone that, becoming truly mobile, had slid out of the bottom of his trouser leg.

'Why don't you get a new pair of trousers?' I asked, before I could stop myself. I knew this was not the time for petty carping. His look said as much. I tried to make amends with a brilliant suggestion, 'Let's look for the key.'

We looked around and our hearts sank. The car park was huge, stretching over a few acres, and was the reason why my husband had agreed to attend the wedding in the first place. Parking is always a sensitive issue with him, but when he heard the name of the venue, he had brightened, even though it meant a long drive.

'Wait a minute,' soothed my friend, 'let's not get worked up.' Turning to my husband, she said, 'First, the key question. Where do you think it could have fallen?'

'That's exactly what I'd like to know,' he rejoined, rolling his eyes, his patience wearing thin at our unhelpful suggestions.

'Let me do a recap,' he said and mused while we stared hard at the road, willing a key to pop up miraculously. 'I had the key when I got out of the car,' he began. 'Obviously,' I commented and was hushed by my friend. My husband went on, 'I put it in my pocket, then walked to the hall, went in with both of you, found seats...'

'Changed them twice,' I added.

'Waited in a queue,' he continued, ignoring my interruption, 'before going to the stage to greet the bride and groom, walked to the dining hall for lunch, came out and, well, here we are.'

'Which means everywhere!' I groaned. The impossibility of the task hit me. Even the proverbial needle in the haystack would have been easier to find. And the hall was too far from the city to go home by auto for the duplicate key.

We decided to re-trace the path we had taken since stepping out of the car. 'Let's split and look for the key,' my husband suggested. 'I'll take baby steps from where I'd parked the car to the entrance of the hall while you search inside.'

'Gladly!' I responded. It was blazing hot outside. Who would want to take steps—baby or giant—there? Glasses perched on our noses, the better to scan the floor with, the friend and I set out, heads bent, inviting curious glances from the guests with the action replay of our peregrinations. Sherlock Holmes would have given us an approving nod, so minutely did we examine the floor of the route taken earlier.

We traipsed to our seats, looked under them, zigzagged our way to the stage, bumping into people, and wished the newlyweds again, our downcast eyes making us look more demure than the bride. We asked the ushers, photographers and event management staff if they had spotted an unclaimed key. Our host offered to arrange a car for us, but that wouldn't solve our problem.

The people in the dining hall were more helpful. The person in charge impressed upon us the honesty of his staff. 'They will hand in even a pin that's found,' he asserted. I wondered if I should bring up the fact that I had actually lost a hairpin but felt this might not be the occasion to mention it.

The servers and cleaners were told to look under, on and around tables and stools. An enthusiastic search had just begun when my phone rang. It was my husband playing spoilsport by calling to say the key had been found—in the lost and found section. Somebody had handed it in.

I couldn't believe there was such a convenience at the venue; what a sophisticated set up! But I have to confess, I felt a bit let down. I would much rather the key had been discovered at the bottom of the pappadam basket.

As my husband opened the car door, he remembered something and asked, alarmed, 'The house key?'

'Safe in my purse,' I proudly replied.

JUST WHAT THE DOCTOR ORDERED

Nerves of Steel

EVER TRIED TO SPEAK WITH YOUR MOUTH WIDE OPEN, while someone squirts water in it and tinkers with your teeth at the same time? No, this wasn't a party game or the circus, but something dead serious—an experience at the dental clinic. No doctor inspires as much fear as a dentist; you need nerves of steel to keep an appointment with them, even when they are your good friend. The gloved and masked doctor, the awe-inspiring chair, the array of gleaming equipment, the light overhead and the bin close by, are all calculated to send you into panic mode.

Shakespeare was on target when he said, '...there was never yet philosopher that could endure the toothache patiently.' And when even philosophers can't suffer toothache with equanimity, what would those like me who can't philosophise to resuscitate a dying aunt do? Hold the swollen cheek in anguish, wail and hail the services of a competent dentist, that is what.

The dentist peered into my mouth and his jaw fell on sighting the riches lurking within. My mouth was a practical textbook of dental problems; a dental student's delight. Remnants of previous repairs gone wrong rubbed teeth and gums with new problems.

'Hmm! Cavities, caries, cracks on the cap!' he exclaimed, sounding exultant.

'How alliterative!' I thought, open-mouthed.

He continued like a seasoned detective, 'I see evidence of bridging, filling, capping, extractions…'

'Braces and root canal treatment too,' I added inarticulately.

He began a close examination of my teeth and gums. 'Too much brushing,' he frowned. 'When your brushing leaves you discontented, then it's good for your teeth, but if you feel satisfied with your brushing, it isn't good.' I was baffled. That Shakespearean philosopher who couldn't endure the toothache might have made sense of it, but I spent the rest of the session working it out in my head.

'Too many extractions,' he sounded disapproving. 'One must try to save teeth.'

'Too late,' I slurred. 'Those dental college house surgeons probably practised extraction on my teeth when I was in high school.'

'Tartar!' he cried.

'Where?' I whirled my head, alarmed, visualising an armed warrior in the vicinity.

'Stay still. Tartar. Plaque. On your teeth. They need to be cleaned.' I thought he had just said I brushed too much, but with all those dental tools in my mouth, I was ill-equipped to contradict him. A whirring sound signalled the start of the cleaning procedure. Instinctively I clenched my fists. 'Relax,' he urged.

How do I relax when an intimidating needle has embarked on a conducted tour over my teeth? Any time the drill could touch a nerve and send shock waves down my nervous system. As if on cue, it did. 'Ah!' I winced in pain. 'Ha! You have sensitive teeth!' His tone was almost congratulatory. 'But don't move, your tongue will get cut,' he cautioned. That worked and I froze like a wax model.

An X-ray confirmed I needed root canal treatment and he scheduled it for the following Friday, showing his excellent teeth in an endearing grin to inform me it would be a very lengthy procedure, as if a delightful picnic was in store.

On Friday, once the anaesthesia took effect, he began the carpentry work. The machine sounded like a saw hewing through my teeth. 'The bridge has to be broken,' he explained. Breaking bridges is no mean feat. I was impressed and decided to cooperate, an easy decision, for the right side of my mouth was numb, but I could still sense the sawing and the levelling, the probing and the prodding that was going on.

Plonk! A fake tooth fell. 'We'll make a new bridge. Not silver this time, but your tooth's colour. Natural.' 'White? I asked, hopefully. 'No, the exact same colour of your tooth. Yellow.' I had asked for that. The whole procedure took ages and finally, jaws stiff, I crawled away with another appointment fixed.

Once the bridging was done, I thought it was all over. 'You can chew anything except gum. And after meals, prise out the food particles lodged between your teeth,' the dentist advised.

'I always do. With a safety pin,' I smiled.

'Pin?' He was horrified; his tone indicated he had finally discovered the reason for the poor state of my teeth. 'Use a tooth pick. And wait, I need to repair a cracked tooth.'

So there I was, mouth open again, water being squirted in and an instrument drilling into my tooth. 'The crowning is next week.'

It isn't always queens who are crowned. But I couldn't even say, 'Wow!'

Half a Worm is Better than None

I CUT OPEN A BRINJAL AND OUT POPPED A WORM. 'HELLO, there!' it appeared to say, lifting its tiny head quizzically and moving it this way and that, trying to size up its surroundings. I could swear it was squinting at the sudden brightening of its world. 'Hello to you too, you beautiful, organic creature. Glad to meet you,' I replied, elated.

The joke that goes, 'What's worse than finding a worm in the apple you are eating? Half a worm,' doesn't hold good any more. Things have taken a U-turn and finding half a worm in the fruit into which you have sunk your teeth is cause for celebration. It is immaterial which part of the worm you have consumed; all that matters is if the worm could eat the fruit and survive, at least till you bit its head or tail off, so can you. It's all about going organic, the buzzword now.

Those days are gone when you ignored heaps of grapes that had flies buzzing around them and made a beeline instead for those fruits that appeared fresh, pristine pure and relatively untouched by insect kind. Going by colour, shape and size, you carefully selected seasonal and unseasonal fruit, according to the contents of your purse, not cottoning on to the fact that the luscious, golden-yellow mangoes, the round, attractive oranges, the dignified bunches of royal purple grapes, the shiny red apples, the unblemished green and yellow guavas, the pretty plump plums, the firm, brown sapotas and of course the wide range of colourful bananas owed their pin-up looks to a generous helping of chemical preservatives.

When the chemical preservative bubble burst, it left the vegetarians dismayed. I remember my vegetarian friend cautioning me against eating meat, fish and eggs. 'Injected with antibiotics,' she had hissed. 'And chock full of hormones.' 'Excellent!' I had replied. 'Now I can get antibiotics for free and also escape hormone therapy.' 'Don't joke about such serious matters,' she frowned in disapproval before harping on her pet theme, 'Listen to me, turn vegetarian. Eat vegetables and fruits. They are healthy and safe.' It is every vegetarian's mission in life to convert non-vegetarians to their ilk.

'Now what do you have to say?' I asked her, armed with facts and statistics about the chemical assault on fruits and vegetables. She heard me out in silence and when I had finished educating her, rallied to say, 'But you're still worse off than us, for you eat vegetables and fruits too.' She had me there.

'I'm going organic,' she announced. 'Come, let's go shop for authentic, organic stuff.'

The principle that what's good for insects and other creatures is bound to be good for humans influenced our purchases as we ferreted about for stale buns, mouldy cakes and crumbling biscuits. We bought rice kept in a sack under which a lizard disappeared and flour kept in another from which a startled cockroach jumped out. I drew the line at green gram that contained stuff which looked suspiciously like rat droppings until my friend nonchalantly waved my objection aside saying the government allows a certain percentage of droppings and crushed insects in farm produce. 'Wash it well,' was her advice.

We went to the fruit market and buzzed like flies around those fruits that had an additional topping of insects. 'Wow! Look at that!' my friend exclaimed in delight. 'So many flies and ants on the fruits sold by the seller in the corner! Let's buy from him.'

'Pssst!' whispered a fruit seller who had been eavesdropping. 'That man's a crook. He sprinkles his fruits with sugar syrup to attract insects. And see that department store that advertises its pure, organically grown vegetables and fruits? I know from where the stuff comes. Organic, my grandmother's swollen left foot! They add pesticides on the sly and hike the price. People are prepared to pay through their nose to buy good health. Buy from me. I don't use pesticides. My fruits have worms. Good protein. Look.' He cut a mango and a small beetle flew out.

'The only solution,' suggested my friend, 'is to grow your own vegetables.'

'We are trying that, anyway,' I replied. 'But we haven't got any produce yet.' My husband had started a kitchen garden on the terrace using manure made from our own vegetable waste. There was an endless supply—every alternate day I handed him a bag or two, and sometimes even three.

'Be patient,' she advised. 'Anything organic takes time.'

The next morning my husband gifted me the first brinjals from our terrace garden...

Gym Eves

'CAN YOU LOSE WEIGHT SELECTIVELY?' I ASKED A FRIEND who is a doctor. 'I mean, just the weight around your stomach?'

'Flab, you mean,' she said.

'Er, yes, you can say that,' I responded, the image of a shapeless whale filling my mind immediately. For some odd reason, I link the word flab with blub or blubber and by association, the robust whale.

'No, you can't,' she continued to be brutally frank. 'Even if you lose weight overall, you could still end up with a tummy. But,' she added, by way of consolation, 'even Marilyn Monroe had a tummy. Everyone has a tummy. It's unnatural not to have flab around the stomach.'

'Then what about all those gorgeous models with midriffs that resemble flat boards?' I asked.

'They are actually holding their breath,' she replied. Oh, really? Superhuman creatures. Where can you learn to hold your breath like that?

At the gym, of course. Or at yoga classes. I remembered an acquaintance describing how she learnt to hold her breath for short periods at the gym while lifting weights and for longer periods at her yoga classes. 'Still walking?' she had scoffed, strolling towards her car. 'Outdated. Not to mention lonely, boring and risky. Gym or yoga, these are the only options.'

The gym thing became the in thing while practically everyone went gaga over yoga. All the hype and the hoopla about lifestyle diseases and the need for active exercise sent people scurrying to these for succour. Sedentary adults who had lived a car-to-carpet lifestyle struggled to their feet in shock when every newspaper supplement they ran their lazy eyes over, urged them to lead energetic, healthy lives or else...

The doomsday prophesy sent them shuffling to enrol themselves in the best gym. Distance was no problem. Cars would take them there and lifts would deposit them on the right floors. Yoga and meditation, gym and workouts became the mantra of every health freak.

I too fell under the spell and began to toy with the idea of trying a yoga position on my own. I love the lotus pose and quite fancied myself seated cross-legged, hands on my knees, a serene expression on my face as I breathed in and out deeply. But my first concern was what to wear—a woman's eternal problem. I looked it up on the internet and was amazed. Apparently, snug, scientifically engineered compression garments are a must for yoga, gym or even a walk. To think that all these years I had been walking wearing the wrong stuff!

My head reeled when I read about how the right fitness clothes 'apply a balanced pressure on different parts of the body, which in turn accelerates blood flow and helps our muscles work.' Next I read, 'Tight clothes enhance performance.' Wow! I took a closer look and found to my disappointment, it was right clothes, not tight and by performance they only meant exercise. I was also urged to go in for all-season friendly, anti-bacterial material to help avoid body odour, and to wear the right shoes, of course.

Why, I had discovered a short cut to good health—just wearing these clothes would do the trick. Elated, I checked the price, balked and decided to stick to the good old all-season, all-purpose sweaty salwar kameez.

I tried to sit cross-legged on the floor with my feet resting on the opposing knees and promptly toppled backwards. I tried again and got cramps on my legs and a shooting back pain. My breath coming in gasps, my face contorted with pain, I stumbled to the bed to lie in a supine position till the cramps disappeared. But the back pain lingered.

No more lotus position for me, I decided. I was going in for a real workout—stretching, aerobics, and strength training—to improve my quality of life. It would reduce BP, stress, lower my heart rate, anxiety and insomnia, keep my bones strong and render me fit and flexible.

After my failed yoga experiment at home, I decided going to the gym would be safer. From my friend I learnt that the sessions were at 5 in the morning. What?? That was enough to raise my heart rate and my BP, give me stress, anxiety and insomnia. A heavy price to pay, especially when I learnt from my friend, who was now wearing a collar for spondylosis, that workouts could be harmful too.

That settled it. I'm back to walking. When I next met my doctor friend, she looked critically at me and exclaimed, 'Why, you don't have much flab!'

I couldn't reply. I was holding my breath.

The New Smoking

'SITTING IS THE NEW SMOKING.'

Holy smoke! I said to myself the first time I read this news item that has been doing the rounds for a while now. I instinctively sat up; then hastily stood up to read the rest of the article, quite like the policeman in the movies who jumps up and stands at attention when he gets a call from his superior. The contents impressed me. This needs a standing ovation, I thought.

I decided to spread the word and sprang it on a friend who is a sitting duck for all the physical ailments the article promised. She is one who believes that legs are merely decorative appendages, to be used as sparingly as possible. She didn't respond like I had done—springing up is an exertion alien to her temperament. In fact, she didn't stir; she merely looked up at me, puzzled. Yes, you guessed right; she looked up because I was standing like an impatient prophet of doom before her. 'You mean it is as pleasurable?' she asked lazily.

'Pleasurable? Ha! You must be smoking, I mean, joking,' I replied. 'Sitting is as DANGEROUS as smoking. Just listen...'

I reeled off whatever I could remember—sitting for a prolonged period slackens the body's metabolism, causing the lipo-whatever enzyme which breaks down our body's fat reserves to botch up its function. Meanwhile, inactivity also prompts the body's blood pressure and blood glucose levels to rise and ultimately you end up with diabetes, heart ailments and even cancer. Obesity and poor posture are the additional perks. Not a cheerful prospect at all.

She refused to believe me. 'It's normal to sit. People have been sitting happily for ages,' she protested. 'And dying like flies,' I added theatrically. It took some effort, but finally I managed to convince her that sitting for long is indeed fatal. 'Research has proved it,' I said, with the ring of authority. 'And the World Health Organisation says physical inactivity is the fourth biggest killer on the planet.' Now she looked agitated and exclaimed, 'But I've always sat! It's part of being comfortable.'

'What is sat cannot be unsat,' I said ungrammatically. 'But it's never too late to make amends. You've got to spend more time on your feet than in your seat. And your time starts now.'

But she was right—sitting indeed contributes hugely to your comfort. Asking guests to be seated is a prerequisite of good etiquette, of putting them at ease. And you're always looking around for seats or booking them—whether you're visiting, travelling, going for a movie or attending a programme. The sofa, the settee, the bench and the chair are part of the furniture in any drawing room, waiting room, classroom or workplace.

How weird is this? You take advantage of various inventions to make yourself comfortable, read inactive—mobile and cordless phones to render you immobile, vehicles to transport you to your place of work or wherever you wish to go, lifts or escalators to take you to different floors, chairs to sit on as you work or relax, cosy settees in front of the TV to make you snug as you transform into a couch potato, munching potato chips...

And just when, smartphone in hand, you think smugly that life is one lazy, idyllic picnic, there comes this alarming assertion—sitting is the new smoking.

You realise, too late, the merits of the life you led before, when you ambled to the bus stop, got into a crowded bus by elbowing your way in—quite some art, that—and stood throughout the journey, alighted and walked briskly to your workplace, ran up several flights of steps to reach your office where, perhaps, you did sit down. But your work kept you in regular touch with human beings, not machines; and human beings have the knack for making you jump to your feet constantly.

Interestingly, it is believed that women live longer than men because the housework they do keeps them on their feet. Alas, in their fight for equal rights, they are squandering this vital advantage over men; their desk jobs are making them as vulnerable as men to lifestyle diseases.

Milton knew what he was talking about when he said, 'They also serve who only stand and wait.' Or maybe he should have said, 'They serve best who only stand and lose weight.'

The Appeal of Vegetable Peels

I WOKE UP ONE MORNING WITH PUFFY EYES. NOTHING new, this swollen condition of the eyes; it happens whenever I stay up late the night before, gazing into the computer screen. On that day they looked worse than usual, as if some ants had joined in the fun and aided the swelling by injecting formic acid there.

The voice of cosmetic education told me, 'Put some potato peels under your eyes and on your upper lids too.' I had just packed a healthy lunch for my husband, with a variety of fresh vegetables, and seen him off. Now all those vegetable peels lay in a vibrant heap on the kitchen counter, looking invitingly at me as if to say, 'Use us.'

Why not, I thought, especially since I had got my puffy eyes reading about the benefits of using vegetable peels on one's face, the previous night. It was only poetic justice that I should put to use my newly acquired knowledge of organic ways to get rid of facial blemishes.

'Organic', 'pure' and 'natural' are the buzzwords of today. Everyone's talking healthy and trying to eat healthy. Awareness has spread about the dangerous levels of chemicals in the environment, water, food, medicine and cosmetics. Quick to cash in on people's desire to go green and eat 'real' food and not processed junk, multinational companies have initiated an organic rush.

People flaunt bottled mineral water, never mind that sometimes it is just local tap water that gets bottled. Not a bad thing after all, for the microorganisms they imbibe might improve their resistance. The labels 'organic', 'farm fresh' or 'pure' for products ensure quick sales of everything, from grains to eggs and even chyawanaprash. Who reads the fine print anyway?

As for cosmetics, they are almost always labelled 'herbal' and made from fruit or vegetable extracts and sometimes tea. Ayurvedic soaps vie with soaps bursting with vitamins, minerals and antioxidants for the customer's attention while hair oil and shampoos made from natural ingredients are touted to take hair to the proverbial strength of Samson's.

I decided to experiment. As I gently placed the potato peels over my eyes, I remembered that cucumber slices would do the trick too, and they had the added advantage of having the right shape to stay on eyes. Undeterred by the fact that I had only peels, not slices, I carefully arranged long scrapings over the potato peels.

I remembered reading that tea bags too were supposed to be good for removing the bags from under your eyes, so why not that too, for good measure? The article hadn't said anything about using a fresh or a used tea bag, but there was no way I was going to waste a new one. Since there was only one used tea bag, my husband preferring a cup of coffee in the morning, I let it hang by the thread over my right eye to cover it, pirate-like, and rest lightly on the lower lid.

I considered the carrot peels that were lying on the counter. Aha, a dash of colour would be great. I recollected that carrot peels are best for nourishing the skin, so I piled them on. Ooh na, na, no banana? The lone banana skin looked tempting as its benefits played on my mind. I balanced the stem on the bridge of my nose, allowing the sections of the skin to flow longitudinally down. And how could I have forgotten the citrus merits of the lemon peel, left behind after the squeeze of lemon on the salad? The only free part of my face was the tip of my nose and I capped it with the peeled lemon.

Satisfied with the way I had temporarily transferred all the biodegradable vegetable waste from my kitchen counter to my face, I decided to drink a few glasses of water, also believed to aid in reducing puffiness. I was downing the third glass while delicately balancing the scraps on my face when the doorbell rang. I peered cautiously through the grill and saw my husband. He had returned, as he explained later, for a book. What he saw, though, was a weird, inhuman face that seemed to have walked straight out of a C-grade horror film. He paled. What monster had strayed into his peaceful, quiet house? 'Eek! Help!' he yelped, but as he turned on his heel to escape, I found my voice. 'Hey, it's me,' I said ungrammatically.

Once he had recovered from his shock, he gave me a disapproving once over and asked, 'Why don't you try soap and water?'

Now all the vegetable peels go straight into the garbage bin.

DIY MISADVENTURES

A Tyre-ing Job

I DON'T FANCY CARS MUCH, BUT I'VE ALWAYS BEEN FASCINATED by the idea of changing tyres—probably a throwback to old Hindi movies where a flat tyre acted as a catalyst for a romance. A typical scene pans out this way: the heroine's car crawls to a halt in the middle of nowhere, the annoyed heroine stomps out and, to give her credit, identifies the problem after circling around the car making squeaking noises. A rear tyre is punctured.

'Hmf!' she squeals in dismay and pouts helplessly. As if on cue, the happy-go-lucky hero appears, again out of nowhere. The heroine looks at him as if he is a bad smell and turns up her nose at his wisecracks and overtures. Now he resorts to what he knows best. He bursts into a zippy, catchy number as she sashays off in a huff. He prances after her in erratic circles like a hyper-active Mary's lamb, dancing as though he has ants in his pants.

The song fades out; he sobers down and changes the tyre, practically with his bare hands, a hero's prerogative. Annoyance gives way to admiration. She flashes a coy smile, he leaps into the driver's seat, she gets in from the other side and they drive off to nowhere in particular. Love has blossomed and a flat tyre has set it into motion.

The front tyre of our car was punctured, a friend pointed out with glee. Sure enough, it was deflated and looked down in the dumps. 'How?' I was curious. 'It was fine yesterday.'

'These things don't give a two-week warning,' my husband muttered, examining the tyre. 'I'm going to change it.'

'You are?' I was most impressed. I didn't know he had these skills. 'Did you learn from old Hindi movies?' There was silence. A sudden phone call took my attention but from the corner of my eye, I could see him go back and forth purposefully, carrying first a jack, then a wrench and finally the toolbox. After a few such journeys he disappeared. I quickly ended the call and raced to the front room. The car manual was lying open on the floor and he was devouring it, frowning in concentration.

A little later I followed him outside. I found the car jacked up; obviously he had decided to consult the manual after that. Now he lugged the spare tyre to the scooter parked close by. He was sweating and whispered, 'Air, air'.

'Breathe through your mouth,' I said, alarmed.

'Nonsense, I'm going to check the stepney's air pressure,' he retorted in his normal voice and left, the tyre balanced precariously on his wobbling scooter.

He returned soon. 'The tyre's fine. Now bring some stones.' Stones to change a tyre? Didn't make sense but I obeyed and offered gravel. 'Gravel? Are you crazy? Fetch some big stones.'

'Aren't you getting under the car?' I asked. 'That's what heroes generally do.'

'If you don't get those stones, I'll be knocked under all right,' he snapped.

Now I got it. The stones were to prevent the car from rolling when the tyre was being changed. With great difficulty, I lugged two boulders to the car. He was exasperated. 'Too big.' I heard him mutter, 'Self-help is the best help.' He went off to choose the stones himself. He then propped the stones under the tyres and painstakingly unscrewed the lug nuts that held the rogue tyre in place.

He waved aside my offers of assistance and after much grunting, panting and sweating, got the tyre off with a jerk, tumbling back in the process, legs cycling in the air. Now was my time to shine. I sprang to lift the tyre and recoiled with a yowl of pain almost immediately, kicking the nuts all over the place. How was I to know there are tiny wires on worn-out tyres that stand out like treacherous barbs? By now he had regained his balance and prepared to start work but some nuts were missing. I disappeared too.

I returned only when the last nut was in place. What ought to have taken ten minutes had taken an hour. But my husband looked relieved that his reputation as a changer of tyres remained intact. I discovered a tiny screw near the door. 'Here's a screw,' I said. 'From your head?' he laughed. 'Now bring the bags.' He got in behind the wheel while I tripped over the flat tyre and leapt into the passenger seat, strewing the bags about. And we drove off to somewhere in particular—the vegetable market.

Losing Sleep over Waste

WHEN A SMART GIRL CAME KNOCKING ON OUR GATE ONE morning to say she was going to collect garbage from the houses in our neighbourhood, I almost kissed her. At last we could breathe easy and sleep peacefully. The city has been struggling to solve the garbage problem ever since the waste disposal plant was shut down almost four years back. The simplest solution for many people was to stuff garbage down gutters or throw it on the roadside, converting our clean city into a glorified dump with a musty aura hanging over it.

The amount the girl quoted was large by garbage collection standards, but I felt she was perfectly entitled to command the price for the sterling service she was offering to render. And for every day of the week. 'Even on Sundays?' I asked, open-mouthed. 'Yes,' she bobbed her head with enthusiasm. Wow, no day wasted. She must love her job. Gratitude surged through me; I would gladly have given double the amount if she had asked.

Her instructions to me were simple: 'Keep the biodegradable waste and plastic waste in separate bags. I'll come every morning.'

'What time?' I asked, a little alarmed. I share my sleep pattern with the owl.

'Seven,' she replied.

'How about seven-thirty?' I suggested. She agreed willingly and added she would whistle to announce her arrival.

Did I say we could breathe easy and sleep peacefully at last? Ha! I had no clue about the girl's plans.

The first few days everything was a breeze. She came regularly and on time, whistling like a train with a sore throat, and whisked the garbage away. Then, one morning, I found the bag still resting against the gate. I thought she might have taken ill. But my neighbour said she had collected the garbage from her house. 'She came earlier than usual,' my neighbour clarified. 'She whistled and banged on your gate too.'

The sleepless nights began. She delighted in coming at unearthly hours. Her whistle would make my husband leap from the bed to unlock the gate while I would leap to the kitchen for the waste, sealing the contents in the bag with a rubber band as I galloped to the gate only to find her gone. In the beginning I would place the bag in its allotted position anyway, hoping optimistically she would come on a second round. I couldn't believe everyone in my locality got up so early. I was sure she had a second beat for the late risers.

But it appears I was mistaken. She didn't come back. Then she stopped coming on Sundays and began to take days off in between. We lived in uncertainty. Any stray sound in the night sounded like a whistle to us, and we woke up at odd hours to unlock the gate for the garbage ritual. Garbage took over our sleeping and waking hours—we thought garbage, we dreamt garbage. I appealed to my husband to go back to his natural composting with all our vegetable waste. 'No way,' he said, 'no more pots left.'

'Do something,' I begged. 'Anything, to relieve me of this "Will she? Won't she?" uncertainty.'

Last week I found her waiting for me, tapping her foot to show her impatience. She said she planned to collect the waste from five in the morning the following day onwards. 'Five?' I was dumbstruck. She must be crazy.

'Keep the bag on the gate's pillar the previous night,' she suggested. 'A few houses are already doing it.'

'But we have dogs around who are champion high jumpers,' I protested, 'and rival cats that congregate on the pillars for raucous music competitions.'

'Then cover it with a bucket,' she said and left.

My husband was appalled. 'What do you mean, put a bucket on the newly painted pillar of our newly painted gate?'

I clarified I'd only use an old paint bucket. That incensed him further. 'A DIRTY bucket garnishing garbage on my pillar? Keep the bag outside.'

'That would still attract the creatures of the night,' I said. I assured him his precious pillar would lose its dignity only for a few hours of the night. 'Who's going to look, anyway?'

'What about the early morning joggers?' he persisted.

'They have better things to gaze at than dirty buckets,' I retorted. 'Other joggers, for instance.'

So now a bucket hides the garbage bag on the pillar. The overhanging roof protects it from rain. We sleep peacefully. And take the garbage back in the next morning, along with the bucket. For she hasn't collected it.

The Gentle Art of Washing Up

'YOU HAVE HYDROMANIA,' SAID MY HUSBAND, ENTERING the kitchen as quietly as a cat and startling me into dropping a steel lid. 'And you have hydrophobia,' I retorted. Once these endearments had been exchanged, he wrenched the scouring pad from my hand and ordered me out of the kitchen to take up the dish washing from where I had left off.

When I finish the dishes, the kitchen looks as if several crows have had a satisfying bath there. Water is splashed all around, often dripping off the counter to the floor. In vain I tell my husband not to come upon me while I'm still in the process of washing up. When done, I wipe the place so dry no one would believe it had resembled a miniature swimming pool a little while before. But no, he'll come just when I'm warming up to my task, hands sloshing around inside the sink with water gushing out full force from the tap and bouncing off the plates to spray in all directions.

'It's criminal, the way you waste water,' he remonstrated, turning the tap off to a trickle, disapproval dripping from his voice like the water from the tap. 'See, this is the right way to do it.' He proceeded to demonstrate his washing up skills, gently taking a plate I had lathered rather too well and holding it under the tap. I waited impatiently for what seemed like an eternity as he rinsed it in slow motion and then left him to do the rest at his own pace.

My husband can't cook but he loves washing up—when he has the time, that is. For he needs plenty of time and leisure, his methods being very slow, measured and thorough.

We have a music system in the kitchen and to the accompaniment of music that ranges from European classical and Carnatic veena to hard rock and folk music, most of which is meant to keep me out of the kitchen, he washes up at the same leisurely tempo, contentment writ large on his face.

My modus operandi while washing up, on the other hand, is slapdash. For me, doing the dishes is the necessary but undesirable culmination of the task of cooking and the idea is to finish it as quickly as possible. Water leaps out of the tap and under my frenzied guidance, dishes clang against one another, spoons rattle and glasses clink, keeping time to the fast-paced music I play, which could be The Beatles at their noisy best or Mohammed Rafi belting out zippy Shammi Kapoor numbers.

This kind of expeditious washing up has its drawbacks, described in great detail by my husband when he takes over. Wearing his glasses and examining every piece of crockery and cutlery with an eagle eye, he begins his nitpicking. 'Look at the stain on this plate and the grime on the spoons! And there's dirt in every ridge of this glass. Why don't you buy plain glasses and plates instead of these fancy, cutwork types? So difficult to keep them clean.'

My protest that they are gifts cuts no ice with him. 'Tell your friends to give you sensible presents. And the glasses wouldn't have got so dirty if you had your glasses on when you washed them. Where's the toothbrush I'd kept here? And the metal scour pad?'

The cleaning fetish gets hold of him and when the washing up is over, he progresses to the other items in the kitchen. Once he's done, the kitchen looks as if it has got a facelift. If the mood continues, he makes a foray into the storeroom and in spite of my protests that some of the pots and pans there are old and damaged, he resurrects them into shining pieces of scrap metal, much to the bafflement of the junk dealer.

My friends wish their husbands would take a scrubbing leaf out of my husband's book. A friend who is a beneficiary of his magic with dish-washing is especially admiring. The other day, she sent him food when I was out of station and when he returned the containers, she almost refused to take them back for they were gleaming beyond recognition. 'How wonderful it would be,' she sighed after I returned, 'if all my shabby containers could get to look this good.'

'They could,' I said. 'Keep sending us food in them.' I smacked my lips in anticipation. She is an excellent cook.

Rule of Thumb

THERE ARE MANY WAYS OF GREETING PEOPLE YOU HAVEN'T seen in years; mine was by jumping out of the car and slamming the door on my thumb. Ooff! This just goes to prove you don't need anybody's help to orchestrate a disaster; you only need that bit of extra something, that special knack for it.

I had arrived for a school programme and the sudden sharp pain from my jammed thumb shot up my arm like a surge of electric current. I freed my thumb with a quick tug, gave my wildly gesticulating friend a big hug and proceeded to meet the others, though the injured thumb kept demanding attention by radiating painful signals. As we walked into the building, I looked down casually at my right hand and found the injured nail had changed to an ugly colour. Eek! Grey, or was it bluish-black? Whatever it was, it looked serious and I drew a teacher's attention to it. In no time, a tumbler full of ice cubes, sponsored by the chemistry lab, made a magical appearance. Hurray for chemistry labs! 'Put your thumb right in,' I was advised. I obeyed—I'd have kissed the ground if I'd been told that would help the pain disappear—and twiddled my thumb in the glass till the programme began.

As the session got under way, I had to part with the tumbler, to which I'd got quite attached, and forget about my pain. After all, you can't have the speaker twiddling her thumbs during her speech, can you? But I couldn't help sneaking the occasional glance at my nail to see what colour it had turned. It was changing hues in a fascinating manner—all colours of the rainbow and a few more besides. It switched from a dignified greyish-blue to a pedestrian brown to an intriguing violet-indigo to a yucky green to a brilliant turquoise blue to a bizarre combo of yellow, red and orange, finally settling down to a dull black with a pink, healthy spot in a corner.

When my session was over, it was time for lunch and I decided to go vegetarian—it's easier to scoop herbivorous morsels when you have only four fingers to grip the spoon. I ignored the throbbing during the afternoon's programme but once I was home, the pain returned with a burning intensity. The whole thumb was black, swollen and hot to the touch.

Advice on what to do came thick and fast from all quarters. Place it in cold water, no, hot water. Pack salt around it or better still, keep it immersed in salt water overnight (with a little chilli, perhaps? A pickled thumb!). Try sugar solution, it works better. Just apply some ointment. Tie a bandage around it. Go for a band-aid. No, leave it open, it should be aired. I felt like a mattress on hearing that one. Dismissing suggestions on what I ought to have done as soon as the incident had taken place, I decided to follow the rest. 'Leave nothing to chance,' became my guiding principle as I put my thumb through the third degree.

I quickly realised I hadn't done anything unique or spectacular by smashing my thumb. The whole world, it appeared, had jammed thumbs, fingers, toes, sometimes two or three at the same time, making my feat pale in comparison.

I heard horror stories about how these accidents had happened and the frightening repercussions.

The lady who delivers milk, narrated how a neighbour had banged the door shut on the ironer who had his fingers on the hinge. It was not to show his displeasure at the quality of the ironing, but by sheer accident. The ironer's cries, she said, rang to the next district. He needed surgery in Tamil Nadu, had several stitches put in and was out of action for two months. 'Why Tamil Nadu?' I asked. I thought our medical care was good enough. Because he hails from there, she told me. Ah!

Well-meaning friends cheerfully fed me ghoulish predictions regarding the future of my thumb—it could become partially numb, it might remain black forever, the nail would come off but might not grow back...I looked nervously at the abused appendage. The nail gave a hollow sound when I tapped it. I hadn't shown it to a doctor yet. My husband took a close look and made a profound statement: 'Many things are happening underneath it.'

I obsess over the nail now, examining it minutely for day-to-day changes, though I am also getting used to it. I think it's finally coming off. It looks as though I've used some atrocious nail polish on it, the sort girls seem to favour these days. Someone asked me why I'd painted only one nail. 'It's the latest trend, haven't you heard?' I replied.

TECH AGE HITCHES

Planet of the Apps

NEW YEAR RESOLUTIONS ARE MEANT TO BE BROKEN; THAT'S precisely the reason they are made in the first place, with ditto marks faithfully added at the beginning of every year. No longer, it seems, if you go by the news that there are apps to keep tabs on your resolve. These apps will push and prod you successfully through your resolutions to the bitter end, leaving you a nervous wreck. But not to worry, other apps are waiting around the cyber corner to put the pieces together and make a new, improved you.

Welcome to Earth, the 'Planet of the Apps'—a delightful coinage by a young friend who was tickled when 'apes' was mispronounced 'apps' and then realised he had stumbled upon an apt, need-of-the-hour phrase. Now, Big Brother is not just watching; he's listening, smelling, advising, monitoring and pronouncing verdicts on every little that people do. The American Dialect Society showed great clairvoyance when in 2010 it chose 'app' as its Word (or shall we call it 'Appellative'?) of the Year. Since then the digital stage has been keeping time to the tune of, 'here an app, there an app, everywhere an app app...'

All you need is an Android tablet, an iPad or a smartphone and an app is just a tap away. The smartphone is an 'appening place with apps for every need and for every age—babysitting, education, news, travel, self-help, shopping, sports, games, movies, cookery, fitness... you name it, they have it.

Apps haven't taken over my life for the simple reason I don't have a smartphone. I need a phone only for calls and messages; a simple mobile phone I can rely on. Watching users grapple with the smartphone's strange antics has made me wary of the gizmo. The super sensitive touch screen adds to everyone's woes. It was the stuff of magic when it first appeared; I remember watching wide-eyed as a friend showed off his new smartphone. He touched the screen with a stylus that seemed like a wand; nothing happened. Then he cursed, 'What the... you so-and-so!' and oh, wow, it worked with the effectiveness of an 'Open Sesame.' The cave of spectacular hi tech riches flew open and along with it the liberal spouting of four letter words whenever the smart phone played oversmart.

I remember how once my mobile rang at about three in the morning, alarming us out of our sleep. A phone call at that time can only mean bad news. The best of news waits for a decent hour to be communicated, even if it is to tell you that your mother has won the Nobel Peace Prize or your husband has managed a successful coup and become President of a banana republic. The call was from my son's friend Ajay. Jittery, my husband immediately returned the call, but Ajay didn't respond. He tried three times, and then gave up, but it put paid to our sleep.

In the morning, Ajay asked why we had called three times in the night. 'Any emergency?'

Well, really! 'You called us,' we protested groggily. He acknowledged it could have been his new smartphone's fault—it would call random numbers at any time of the day or night and wouldn't register the calls either. More sneaky than smart, that.

My husband, a reluctant smartphone user, has one with a mischievous mind of its own. It invariably hangs whenever he leaves the city and, sometimes, when he doesn't. Messages get sent when half written and multiple times too, they appear and disappear quixotically. Calls get cut off mid-sentence, videos misbehave, photos vanish .... The other day he lost the names of all his contacts; only the numbers remained. Now he has lost a few friends.

My friends provide me with other experiences. I remember taking a call from a friend—one moment she was loud and clear, the next she was off the air. She later said it was because she had shifted the phone from her left ear to her right. Another friend and her dog worked themselves to a frenzy hunting for a phantom cat that let out piteous meows at strange hours until she realised it was her phone's ring tone, changed to a cat's meowing by her son.

Problems abound and warnings regularly sounded—loading glitches, network and wi-fi malfunctions, charging troubles, radiation fears, addiction, nomophobia... but who cares? Once the Internet of Things or IoT succeeds in linking everyone and everything, will science fiction become fact? Per apps.

Picture Imperfect

THESE ARE DAYS OF GREAT CONVENIENCE WHEN BOOKING train tickets doesn't mean standing in long queues for hours with a book and a packed lunch handy, maybe even a small pillow for a quick afternoon snooze if you expect to spend the better part of the day creeping towards the ticket counter at a speed that would send a snail sniggering into its shell. The option of online booking has taken care of all that but, mind you, it's not always smooth sailing.

The first time I travelled with the details of my train ticket on my mobile, I was pretty apprehensive. When the booking was made I wanted a printout of the ticket, but was told it wasn't necessary; nothing would go wrong as long as I had my ID card with me. But first time jitters continued. What if my temperamental phone decided to stop working? What if its battery died? What if the message with the details disappeared? All these 'what ifs' kept troubling me and I almost greeted the TTE like a long lost friend when he came to my coach half an hour into the journey. Once he checked the ticket, I could relax.

The phone didn't let me down. I located the message and held the mobile under the TTE's nose. He nodded and asked for my ID proof. He took one look at my voter ID card and turned pale, as if he had seen a ghost. He almost had, only it wasn't as much a ghost as a ghoul that glared fiendishly at him from the photo on the card. He jumped back, looking at me with fearful respect. 'That's ...your... picture?' he stammered. 'Yes,' I said, sorely tempted to snarl and imitate my photographic alter ego.

I got my voter ID card years back when the procedure involved going to the polling booth on the date designated to complete the formalities of identification, address proof and other details and get your photograph taken. Now the process is much simpler and easier on the eye too, since you provide the passport size photo. But those who got the cards through the earlier method know that the photos on them, clicked carelessly in a nanosecond, are in a league of their own. They could all jostle for space in the rogues' gallery, no questions asked.

I was appalled when I got my card. Dark, irregular blotches on my cheeks were complemented by light patches in innovative designs on my chin and forehead. My lips were curved in a snarl while my eyes bulged out like a bullfrog's, except that they were fixed in an intense glare. And I had no neck.

The only photos to beat the voter ID specimens are the Aadhaar pictures. When we went to the Aadhaar enrolment centre we heard someone ask if the photos would be as dreadful as those on the voter ID cards. The lady in charge was indignant. 'Never,' she snorted. 'This equipment is much more sophisticated. And we take good care.'

When the cards were delivered home, my husband's card was on top. The greatest care had definitely been taken. One glance at his reinvented mugshot, and my son Amar and I doubled with laughter while my husband stared in horror at his menacing spectacled gaze with his lips curled like a villain's. But Amar stopped with a gasp when his Aadhaar special face popped up from the next card while my husband joined in. Amar's bearded image wore the mother of all frowns while his lips were set incongruously in a pout, 'quite like Marilyn Monroe's,' commented my husband while I wiped tears of mirth from my eyes.

The others hollered and I gulped when it was the turn of my card. For the photographer had reserved his best for me. He had decided that a patchwork complexion suited me best. I had a squint in one eye and a glazed look in the other, like a fish on a slab. My nose, never noticeable at the best of times, was practically missing while my mouth resembled a vampire's. And I still had no neck. Whatever people might say about Aadhaar, there is no denying that its photos have provided much merriment throughout the country. There is no photoshopping here, only photoshocking.

When the TTE almost tossed my voter ID card back and turned away with a shudder, I wished I had brought my Aadhaar card along. Who knows, he might have seen the funny side.

The Aahs and the Ouches of the Computer Age

'YOU HAVE ROTATOR CUFF TEAR,' SAID THE DOCTOR. I WAS A bit taken aback. I had thought I had an aching right arm but now, it turned out, I had something more fancy. 'It could be rotator cuff tendinitis,' he continued. That sounded even more imposing. I never knew I had a cuff in me that could rotate, tear or 'tendinite'. I've always associated cuffs with sleeves, so what's a cuff doing inside me, and rotating at that?

I'm familiar with common troubles like backache, shoulder pain, neck pain and eye strain. For a long time, my husband has been predicting quite a few of the aches and pains bones are prone to. The way I sit, the way I read, the way I type are all wrong, he never tires of telling me. True, I slouch when I sit, curl up awkwardly when I read and slouch and curl up awkwardly when I type.

So when my arm began to ache continuously, alarm bells rang and I began the exercises my husband did for his spondylosis. Yes, with his perfect posture and disciplined ways, he still has spondylosis, don't ask me to explain. When the exercises didn't help, I consulted a specialist.

The doctor explained that the group of muscles and tendons that connects the upper arm to the shoulder joint and supports it, is called the rotator cuff. In simple language, my problem is a muscle tear. I thought only wrestlers and athletes got muscle tears. I follow sports keenly but my love for games doesn't extend to playing them. Could it be sympathetic muscle tear?

A few don'ts were suggested. Don't lift weights was easy; I just had to delegate all the carrying to my husband. Don't reach up for things was difficult for I am short and my cupboards are tall. Do computer work sensibly. Ah, that was almost impossible for I would have to change deeply internalised bad habits. The doctor also prescribed a few exercises for me.

The moment I reached home, I headed straight for the computer and slouched over it to do what else but an intense Google search on rotator cuff tear, while my husband read over my shoulder, seated straight as a ramrod, of course. A doctor friend had once remarked bitterly that the internet is the bane of doctors. Patients no longer come for consultations. They have diagnosed what is wrong, know the treatment and presumptuously tell the doctor what medicines to prescribe.

I learnt that rotator cuff tear could also be a computer-related problem and unblinkingly devoured the details of such problems—MSD (musculoskeletal disorders, not Mahendra Singh Dhoni) and RIS (repetitive stress injury), that include carpal tunnel syndrome, cervical and lumbar spondylosis, tennis elbow and other such exciting names, vision problems, headache and obesity. Other than obesity, I thought I was a sitting duck for the rest.

I heard an 'I told you so'-type of a grunt from my husband when I read aloud, 'Most computer-related health problems are caused by improper use and lack of knowledge about safe computing techniques.' Rotator cuff tendinitis is also called impingement syndrome (how impressive again!) and the article gave tips on how to sit at the computer. 'Sit straight.' I sat straight and, this time, heard an approving grunt in the background.

I was asked to adjust my chair so that the screen would be at my eye level or lower. I brought fat cushions and perched on them like a queen. But the next suggestion stumped me. How do I sit with legs perpendicular to the floor and feet resting flat when my short legs were dangling down from the chair?

Another suggestion was that I use an ergonomic mouse. Eh? I had only heard of chocolate mousse. The next said I should rest my elbows at the sides. Easy. Take mini breaks from work. Gladly! I upped and left the scene.

I have begun the exercises. I draw circles in the air like a low IQ wizard, I bend sideways like a badly positioned wall clock to make pendulum movements with my arm, my fingers crawl up and down the wall like a zombie spider. My husband suggested I hold a dishcloth and choose different surfaces each time I do the last named, to get some cleaning done in the process.

A student who visited me was surprised to see my elaborate seating arrangements. 'Why all this? I just sit any way and type anyhow,' she said airily. 'Don't worry,' I wanted to tell her. 'You'll get there soon enough.'

FUN IN THE CITY

Meetings

'LET'S START WITH A SILENT PRAYER,' ANNOUNCED THE compère at a meeting and the hall livened up. With much scraping of chairs and shuffling of feet, not to mention grunts and gasps, the audience got up, quite loath to abandon contact with their seats. The more generously endowed were unable to abandon contact easily, stuck as they were to their chairs, and needed discreet help to be freed.

The hall had barely fallen quiet when a lady's handbag decided to pitch in with a loud prayer. Jolting everyone out of their piety, it broke into song in a piercing female voice praying for her lost love to come back. The owner dug frantically into her cacophonous bag, but couldn't locate the mobile.

That's the charm of a lady's handbag. Its innumerable compartments have been cleverly crafted to convert every simple search into a complicated detective game. The puzzle regarding which section would yield the desired article is solved, like any good mystery, only when the intensive search is complete. Inevitably it is discovered in the last pouch examined. No woman can complain of boredom as long as she owns such a bag.

All eyes on her, the embarrassed woman decided to escape, hugging her handbag. We could hear the plaintive love song fading in the distance. Lucky woman! I noticed the already flustered speaker direct an envious glance at her retreating back. Someone coughed, another sneezed and, as if in answer to some of the prayers, the compère asked everyone to be seated. More shuffling, scraping and sighs followed and when peace was restored, the speaker was welcomed.

The topic was physiotherapy, the speaker was too soft-spoken and the fans overhead, too loud. I strained my ears to listen to what the young, competent physiotherapist had to say on this interesting subject. The vastness of the topic and the novelty of giving a speech in public made him jittery and he began to race through the definition and history of physiotherapy, mumbling earnestly into his shirt collar.

I gave up listening and looked around, envying my husband who had prudently stayed away. The audience, comprising mostly the middle-aged or elderly, had probably been attracted by the topic, which, no doubt, was very close to their hearts and neuromusculoskeletal systems. But it was no different from an audience at any other meeting, and had already begun adopting survival techniques. Many, including the few young ones who had strayed in, were completely absorbed in their mobile phones—reading or sending messages, watching videos or checking out the innumerable options a smart phone provides—it is a single-instrument entertainer.

Some had sunk into gentle slumber, some into deep sleep —one man almost fell off his chair. A few looked plain bored, some annoyed, staring with hostility at the speaker, while a few others were obviously in another world. Some conducted private conversations in stage whispers, others took calls when their phones rang, rudely loud, making life more stressful for the speaker, while a minuscule group in the front row actually listened. I tried to identify those who must have come with the express purpose of asking a question, or, in the guise of asking one, enumerate their achievements to the audience.

Eventually, the speaker buzzed to a close, wiping the sweat from his forehead. Poised for flight, he asked formally if there were any questions. He got a shock when almost everyone, now miraculously revived, responded with eager nods of their heads and struggled to their feet to ambush him.

The bewildered physiotherapist quickly got the picture—they had all come for a free consultation. An old man began to describe in halting detail his acute back pain that came and went. What should he do? He was cut off midstream by an impatient lady. 'I want to get rid of the swelling on my feet,' she snapped, sticking them out as proof. Someone promptly trod on them to get closer to the physiotherapist and ask why he couldn't bend his right knee fully. He demanded an immediate demo of appropriate exercises to rectify his condition.

Another wanted to know if it was true that physiotherapy could assist people with asthma, diabetes and high blood pressure. 'If it is, please help me,' he wheezed. A young chap sounded outraged that he should have got tennis elbow after playing badminton and insisted on an explanation. I wanted to ask about exercises for my rotator cuff tear, but was pushed out of the reckoning.

The real meeting had just begun.

Getting Inked

'DID YOU GET YOURSELF INKED?' AN ACQUAINTANCE ASKED. 'Inked? Haha!' I laughed. 'A tattoo at my age? How ridiculous I would look!'

'No, no, I wanted to know if you voted,' she responded, sounding impatient. To make herself clear, she stuck the index finger of her left hand up, to show me the indelible ink mark on it. Once again, I muttered a quiet thanks to the EC for choosing the index, and not the middle finger for the purpose, what with newspapers, magazines and social media spilling over with pictures of people showing their inked fingers to the world to establish their credentials as responsible citizens of India.

'Of course I did,' I said, looking ruefully at the electoral ink mark on my forefinger that ran all the way from my knuckle to cover most of my nail. I have hardly ever missed voting, but never had I had so much ink on my hand as proof.

We had gone to the booth at 2 p.m., the best time to vote. No, not because it is an astrologically auspicious time, but because that's when hardly anyone is about. With so many occasions to exercise our franchise—the municipal elections, the Assembly elections and the Lok Sabha elections—everyone seems to have discovered their favourite time slot for the purpose. At one end of the spectrum are those who love to breast the tape first in everything, including voting, and at the other are the stragglers who just about manage to cross the finish line. I favour the middle path and prefer the slack, post lunch-time.

My husband, who has been on election duty fourteen times and at all sorts of places including those with so few facilities he'd have to wake up before the lark to disappear into bushes with a bucket of water, had come to the conclusion that, primitive or sophisticated, people preferred not to forego their siesta even on election days. On his advice, I'd always gone to vote around that time and found he was absolutely right. I would walk in, confirm my identity, hear my name mispronounced, get the electoral vote mark on my finger, vote and return. Voilà!

But this time it was different. Long queues flowing out of the classrooms doubling as booths greeted us, and for the first time I saw gun-toting jawans in battle fatigues haunting the place. They didn't allow anyone to linger after voting, firmly separating wives from husbands, mothers from sons and fathers from daughters. One asked a chap who was reading on his smart phone to put it away and to be smart about it. Another cast a wary glance at the book in my husband's hand.

But that didn't prevent people from airing their views about why the queues, separate for men and women (women's libbers, please note), were long and moving sluggishly. Had everyone grown wise to the fact that 2 p.m. is the slackest hour or was the voter turnout huge this time? Someone suggested that perhaps the ones on duty had closed shop for lunch, which had led to an overload of voters now.

'No way,' declared my husband, his voice ringing with electoral authority. 'The election process is continuous and doesn't allow for breaks.'

'Maybe this booth is manned by women,' another opined, male chauvinism gleaming in his eyes, as the women around him gleefully agreed.

Occasionally, a few people hobbled their way in and marched their way out. 'Who are those, being given preferential treatment?' someone asked, sounding indignant. 'I'm a senior citizen,' a smart 'young' thing giggled and waltzed away. Opinions began to be voiced about how age should not be the only criterion to define senior citizens.

After a forty-five minute wait, my turn came. Once my identity was accepted and my name stumbled over, I signed. Now the manicurist went into action. The lady in charge of inking began to pass the brush over my nail very diligently as if she was applying nail polish, only she moved up to include half my finger too. Back and forth and back again the brush went, until half my finger was encased in indelible ink.

'What's this?' I asked my husband later, drawing his attention to the artistry.

'Silver nitrate,' he replied.

'I meant, why so much ink?'

'To make it impossible for those whose "love" of democracy makes them wish to vote multiple times and under different identities. You must have roused their suspicions, haha!' He responded with misplaced humour.

As I re-examined the decoration on my finger, I realised it was as good or as bad as a tattoo. I was inked in every sense of the term.

Gated Community

I HAD HEARD A GREAT DEAL ABOUT GATED COMMUNITIES and how it's a different world out there, far from the madding crowd. Living in an independent house that's bang on the roadside, I'm used to the noise of continuous traffic, the flow of pedestrians, the occasional raised voices of quarrelling people or drunks on the road. Not to forget the constant intrusions into my house by any passing beggar, conman or salesperson.

There's a sense of connect with the rest of the world, even though every connection renders your purse that much lighter. Hard luck stories melt your heart, sophisticated begging methods fool you into parting with more money than you would care to admit and you clutter your house with a whole lot of useless stuff bought from sad-looking salesmen or motormouth sales girls. Add belligerent stray dogs, snooty cats and occasional piles of garbage, and you get the picture.

The other day I visited a friend who stays in a high-end apartment complex. Entering the forbidding gates, I strode briskly to the entrance where I was stopped by a security guard who regarded me with undisguised suspicion. 'Where do you think you're going?' he asked.

Where did he think I would wish to go except into the complex? I told him I'd come to visit a friend who had a flat on the fourth floor. 'I think,' I added as an afterthought and that made him more sceptical.

'What do you mean, you think? You have to be sure.' I remembered having scrawled the address on a piece of paper and fumbled in my bag for it, finally turning it out on the man's table. As coins, pens, keys, some sticky sweets, a crumpled napkin, some bits of paper, a practically toothless comb, my glasses and mobile came tumbling out, followed finally with a thud by my five-fold umbrella, he looked very annoyed. I ignored him and sifted through the stuff on the table and fell with a 'whoopee,' of joy on the paper with the address.

'401 C,' I declared, sweeping the contents back into my bag. 'Now may I go?'

'Go where, Madam? Write all these details.' He pushed a long book towards me that seemed to require everything from my name to the power of my glasses. 'Where are the columns for my PAN and Aadhaar numbers?' I asked. A bit of sarcasm was quite in order, I felt.

He merely responded with a 'What's your name?' Aha, so he couldn't read! Knowledge of the man's Achilles heel lifted my spirits. 'Your handwriting is illegible,' he sniffed in disapproval. Oops. I gave him my name and the usual question, answer, clarification and reiteration routine that the articulation of my name generates started. Finally he nodded his head and made a call to my friend—'A Currency Note wants to meet you.' I could hear my friend protest, saying she knew no one with such a name, it must be Khyrunnisa, but he persisted, and finally she gave in. Permission granted, he held a card against the door which now opened and I entered the isolated lobby.

The bleak, empty passageways felt spooky, the claustrophobic atmosphere made me uncomfortable and panicking at the thought of taking the lift alone in this eerie place, I decided to use the stairs. But even there I was unsuccessful; I couldn't locate them. So when two boys appeared from nowhere and got into the lift, I scrambled in after them.

My fears disappeared once I entered my friend's cheerful and beautifully furnished flat. She was full of praise for the gated community culture. No more beggars and salespeople ringing the doorbell, a gym, badminton courts and a swimming pool to keep you in shape, a park for children to play...

'The self-contained complex has a system to deliver vegetables and groceries to each apartment. It's peaceful, quiet and dust-free. And well-guarded too,' she ended her panegyric.

Well-guarded! Of course. So well-guarded I was almost denied entry. Getting out proved to be easier and as I was leaving I asked the security guard what his name was. 'Baby,' the burly, moustachioed guard grunted. Haha! A more un-Baby like person would be difficult to find. Life evens things out. I thought that going through a few hours as Currency Note was way better than going through life being called Baby. 'Thank you, Baby,' I laughed and left.

I had just entered my familiar home when the doorbell rang. It was a sly-looking beggar with a sob story. I sighed and went in to get a currency note.

Cats, Rats and Mangoes

WHY IS IT THAT ALL KINDS OF THINGS GET DEPOSITED outside our gate or our compound wall? If it isn't a bag full of chicken refuse— an offal offering, I should add—it is a dead cat. Or a dog chooses to breathe its last there. The other day, the lady from the corporation rang our bell in the morning to announce the demise of a cat whose carcass had been deposited outside our gate, awaiting its last rites. Someone with a wacko sense of humour had fitted the remains into a plastic bag and covered it with gift wrap paper.

This thin, wiry lady was a nice sort whom nature had endowed with a voice that was disproportionate to her size, a voice with the timbre to send cats and dogs bolting to another destination. Unfortunately, she comes upon them only after they are dead. In a tone that carried the news of her discovery to the whole neighbourhood, she said she had arranged for the corporation van to take the decaying cat away. 'That man used his bare hands to scoop it up,' she revealed, lowering her voice to a stage whisper that reached the corporation worker she was pointing at, who grinned and looked down at his bare hands that had doubled as a shovel. I looked at him in awe.

'We do this only for your husband,' the lady made clear. 'He's a good man who offers us tea.' She gave an approving cackle. Who makes the tea? I wanted to ask.

Now she pointed a bony finger at the small heap of garbage on the other side of the road, the responsibility of another corporation ward. Though, under normal circumstances, hired hands of one ward do not raise a finger or lower a broom to help the workers of another ward, she said she would clear it, this once. 'For your husband,' she repeated.

As I'd expected, she wanted a matchbox to set fire to the assorted rubbish and against my better judgement and for want of other options to get rid of the waste, I gave her one. I have them handy, but of course she attributes the supply of them to my husband. 'Tell him I got the matchbox,' she grinned. Leaving her to her incendiary pursuits, I escaped to the kitchen.

A little later she banged on the gate with an urgency and force that threatened to loosen it at the hinges, yelling for me at the same time. This frantic dual summons indicated some calamitous discovery and I reached her at a gallop, all prepared to see a dead horse. 'Look! A dead rat on the opposite side! Big rat!' she exclaimed, eyes shining as if she had come upon a treasure. 'And stinking. Normally we don't clear stuff that is another ward's responsibility but I will do it for…'

'… My husband.' I appropriated her refrain, nodding my head. I had got it. 'Who arranges tea for all of you.'

The corporation man used his bare hands again to transfer the rat to its mobile mortuary. He was tipped generously. My husband appeared at this point and tea was served. The van left soon after and the lady left too, with my matchbox and a broad smile.

Now she faces competition. For the last few days, a young chap selling mangoes has planted himself by the road on the other side of our wall. A catty acquaintance who observed this while passing my house called to ask if I'd taken to selling mangoes now. I hated to disappoint her but confessed it wasn't the case. 'Anybody can use the roadside,' I said. She gave a snort and ended the call.

Given the advantage of an education, the mango guy, with his clear, loud voice, persuasive arguments and energy-sapping persistence in repeating his recital, would have made a good teacher. 'Fresh, native mangoes!' He yells. 'Sweet, tasty and straight from the trees! Have a slice. No pesticides used. Organic.' The word 'organic' is the clincher. Buyers cough up the steep price he quotes, though sceptics swear they smell chemicals on the fruit.

His continuous, ringing sales pitch to every passing pedestrian and vehicle gets on our nerves but it appears to be the price we have to pay for a comparatively clean roadside. Besides, his presence has been a deterrent to animals who wish to rest in peace there.

A subdued corporation lady knocked on the gate. 'There's some garbage at the corner,' she mumbled, pointing a finger into the distance. I turned to get the matchbox. 'Have tea,' said my husband.

KITCHEN BLIPS

Under Pressure

WHICH HOMEMAKER WILL NOT GO INTO RHAPSODIES AT THE mention of a pressure cooker? This excellent labour-, time- and fuel-saving device that is the kitchen god's gift to harried cooks is a most handy possession. But if you're under the impression that it's a very safe device and your most dependable friend in the kitchen, then you better do a re-think, as I did after my scary experience with it. This happened quite some time back, but the episode was so mind-blowing, every detail is etched in my memory as if it happened yesterday.

My innocent looking pressure cooker sat solidly on the fire one morning, not letting on that it was getting ready to chart its wild journey while I made dosas on the other burner. I was totally absorbed in cajoling a particularly stubborn part of the dosa to ease off and terminate its romantic association with the griddle when a tremendous explosive sound rocked the kitchen to its foundations. Shocked out of my wits, I dropped the spatula, and turned towards the direction of the sound. I watched in horrified fascination as the pressure cooker lifted itself bodily, almost magically from the gas stove.

I froze as it went berserk in front of my eyes. It became a rocket, a jet, a flying saucer and a steam engine rolled into one.

It took off, then crash-landed on the kitchen counter, emitting hissing sounds all the while, sounding rather like a thousand bilious snakes spitting out their ire in a bizarre chorus. Then it began its tantric dance. It rocked on its sides, spun like a top and whizzed around in confusion like a piece of sodium in water, all the while ejecting dal like a water sprinkler. It crashed into the wall, hit the stove, banged into the baskets of onions and potatoes and skidded off the counter to the floor, firing on all cylinders. I stood still, heart in mouth, wishing it wouldn't crash into my gas cylinder or my fridge. And, horror of horrors, what if the lid yanked itself off and crashed into me?

My cooker was very old, and had long given up performing the tasks it had been designed for. I believed it was safe, for it neither built up pressure nor retained steam, which would gleefully escape from all sides. Had it surreptitiously been collecting steam all these months for this last hurrah? Had bits of dal lodged themselves here and there, blocking all the outlets? Whatever the reason, it seemed well and truly on the warpath. After that magnificent display of tantrums, it finally managed to force the weight off the lid. A jet of dal spurted out like champagne, hitting the ceiling to create a Salvador Daliesque masterpiece. After a few more spins of steadily diminishing velocity, it finally clattered to a stop.

I surveyed the lentil decorated kitchen. Every nook and corner had dal on it. Spray painting could not have achieved a better result. Surprisingly, my husband and my son did not come darting into the kitchen. The sound ought to have awakened even the dead. Festooned in dal, I marched to the front room and found them engrossed in their respective books. They took one look at me and collapsed with laughter.

Peeved, I told them the cooker had almost burst in the kitchen and hadn't they heard the noise? 'Was that the sound we heard?' asked my husband. He had thought it was a lorry unloading gravel on the road. 'Gravel, my foot. Come and see the kitchen.' They came; my husband took a quick look and asked if the dal would wash off easily. 'Can't afford to get the kitchen painted again,' he said.

He then surveyed the place minutely and delivered a lecture. The kitchen was full of potentially hazardous things, he said, pointing to the gas stove, the mixie, the fridge, the knives, the forks, the ladles … I was alarmed. I did not realise I was spending a great part of my life in such a dangerous environment. It was a comforting thought that at least the cooker would not now be a part of it.

After some months of gas cylinder shortage, heavy electricity bills and a few more lectures, I finally mustered the nerve to go in for a new cooker. But that's as far as my courage will take me. The cooker has only to whistle and I'm out of the kitchen like a shot…

The Cool Saviour

ONAM HAS COME AND GONE, LEAVING BEHIND, AMONG other things, satisfied smiles, expanded waistlines, high sugar levels, empty wallets, weary policemen, mounds of stinking garbage, heavy electricity bills for the government and, yes, fridges stuffed with leftover food.

While everyone else had been planning the menu for Onam, my concerns had fast forwarded beyond the cooking and the feasting to dwell on what to do with the body, or rather, what to do with the food bound to be left over after the elaborate Onam lunch. Indians believe in cooking for a battalion at the slightest opportunity. Where do I store it? You might answer, 'The fridge, of course, silly!' Cool, but then you haven't seen my fridge.

Mine is less a fridge and more a multipurpose repository of all things great and small. The invention of the refrigerator is believed to have changed the world. It changed mine all right. It began by giving me a place where food remained fresh and safe from the many legged rulers of night life in the kitchen. The food's in the fridge, all's right with the world, I'd say as I hit the sack. From storing milk, vegetables, fruits, fish and meat, to progressing to flour, dals, masalas, and then to coffee powder, tea, biscuits, chips and on to medicines, pens, toothpaste, deodorants and nail polish were but small steps. The inventors of the fridge (there are too many contenders for me to name them) would have been stunned at the immense possibilities their invention had opened up. Some people, I believe, even keep their gold there—talk of frozen assets!

Onam's the time for the annual harvesting of my fridge. You'd be amazed at the things it collects and every year is a revelation. My tall, grey and handsome fridge is a prized possession. It was a purchase necessitated when its predecessor, our beloved first fridge, having long outlasted its designated lifespan and been repaired beyond repair, gave up its struggle for existence.

We had been as devoted to it as parents to their firstborn and were loath to give it up. It had served us so well. It taught us magic—how to stretch a single meal over many days. It gave us many practical lessons in physics, chemistry and biology. Solids would change into liquids and then to gas. The process of fermentation became clear especially when gravitation took the fermented batter through two shelves to the vegetable compartment, cleaning which taught me how long it takes for mutated life forms to invade vegetables in cold environs.

It gave us geography lessons too. It had its own frigid zone— the freezer looked like a piece of Antarctica, the icy peaks left no space for any foreign matter. It honed our carpentry skills; we had to chip off the ice in the freezer carefully with a screw driver to make space for stuff.

Its functions started slowly but surely shutting down. Frequent repairs didn't help any longer. There came a time when the freezer, now no longer the home of icicles, was the only cool part and the rest of the fridge became a storage cupboard. Soon even the freezer failed, the wires caught fire. But we needed a shock—which I got when I touched the handle—for us to decide on a replacement.

The excellent tutoring at the hands of the old unreliable made us go in for a big fridge with a huge freezer. We availed of an exchange offer. But one look at our old fridge and the sales agent shook his head. 'Scrap metal. Even that, doubtful.' We bid the beloved scrap metal a tearful farewell and welcomed the smart newcomer into the kitchen.

A sense of adventure took hold of me as I began emptying it before Onam. 'Last year's ginger curry mix!' I exulted, before saner counsel prevailed. Foreign chocolates? Oh no! How could I have forgotten them? Packets of cherries, buried under half opened packets of condiments, vanilla essence, unidentifiable liquids that had begun life as respectable solids and an assortment of things with 'keep in a cool, dry place' on the cover, surfaced. What blind obedience to instructions! Then came the surprise items—a nail cutter, shoe polish, a CD, my husband's glasses, house keys...

The emptied fridge is once again full. I've taken a vow to cook only what is required. The vow is now in my freezer.

The Microwave Rules

MY HUSBAND AND I OFTEN HAVE THESE HIGHLY INTELLECTUAL debates that range from whether it is safer to clean your ears with a toothpick or with a hairpin, or if it is necessary to wash one's hands before eating when you're going to do that after your meal anyway, to whether loudspeakers are louder during political campaigns than during religious festivals or if a microwave oven is more useful than a fridge.

The last named topic became a subject for debate quite recently. As long as the fridge reigned supreme in the kitchen, given its excellent ability to swallow into its magically expanding interior practically anything, including food, there was no question of any competition.

And then came the microwave.

My friends had long been persuading me to get one while my stubborn contention was that heating food on the gas hardly took time and was probably healthier. But one day when the cooking gas got over, the replacement cylinder was nowhere in sight, and, displaying perfectly malicious timing, the electric stove ended its innings with a bang, I whimpered and looked at my husband.

In a few microseconds we made up our minds and in a few more we were at a home appliances store asking for a microwave oven with basic features. 'For heating and eating,' my husband explained to the salesman, cutting short his sales talk. The salesman wasn't pleased but finally found one that suited our requirements. 'Someone will come in the evening for a demonstration,' he told us curtly and washed his hands of us. We bought the oven and ate out.

That evening a technician arrived for the demo. 'Very simple only,' he said. I beamed. The simpler, the better. 'Can I have some water?' he asked. 'Poor man, must have had a long day,' I thought, and brought him a glass of chilled water. He frowned. 'Madam, water to demonstrate how to heat it in the microwave.' He drank it anyway.

I quickly filled the glass from the tap. He placed it in the oven and set the timer. 'Ooof!' he exclaimed when he took the glass out. 'Too hot!' The water bubbled and spilled over his hand. 'What kind of a glass is this?' he asked, holding his hand under the tap. I confessed I had got it for free.

'Don't *buy* anything free, Madam,' he advised. He didn't let me point out the flaw in his statement and continued, 'All third rate only. It could have broken.' I pointed to a crack along one side and said, 'It has.' He grunted, then showed us how to warm some rice after examining the bowl closely. 'Paid for with good money,' I assured him. But before I could get him to heat our dinner, he sensed my intention and beat a hasty retreat.

Microwave misadventures followed. My friend, a great votary of the microwave, came home that night with a classy new bowl and popcorn kernels to celebrate my initiation into the microwave user group. Pop! went the popcorn. Crack! went the bowl, dividing itself neatly into two equal parts; we had put too few kernels and no oil at the bottom. My training had begun.

Another microwave enthusiast gifted me some microwave-friendly plastic containers. My husband frowned. 'No plastic containers. They may be great friends with the microwave but not with our digestive system.' Out they went.

The next day I served my husband puttu heated in the microwave. It fell on the plate with a thunk. Alarmed, I moved away to witness a fascinating duel. He put a spoon to it; it bounced and scampered gleefully to the other end of the plate. He used greater force; the spoon almost split the plate for the puttu had rocketed to another corner. Vexed, he jabbed a fork down to spike it, but it leapt straight for his eye and showing amazing reflexes, he took a blinder of a catch. Reconciling himself to the ineffectiveness of cutlery, he decided to use his fingers to break the puttu but couldn't; it was rock hard. 'Good weapon,' he observed sardonically. 'If Tipu Sultan had had microwaved puttu balls in his arsenal, it would have changed the course of south Indian history.'

The trial and mostly error period included warming cupcakes and almost setting the gadget on fire, getting curries dehydrated to dry sediments, turning chapatis to the consistency of roofing tiles...but finally we got the hang of it.

Now I cook, the fridge preserves, my husband microwaves the food and eats it. Warm food on the table beats everything else. End of debate.

The Gas Man Cometh

'SINGH IS KING, SINGH IS KING, SINGH IS KING...' THE SONG asserting Singh's monarchical status blasted in through the window. 'Well, Singh may be king,' I muttered, 'but the gas deliverer is emperor.' Oh, yes, make no mistake about that. He's the supreme being for whom the whole household waits, putting everything else, however urgent it might be, on hold.

This is obviously a pan-Indian phenomenon, for when we visited a friend in Mohali, I remember how, on hearing the doorbell, she yelled from the bathroom, 'Must be the gas man! Quick, open the door. Don't let him go; I'll be out in a minute.'

The gas cylinder is the thing. Between the receiving of the refill cylinder and the first motion of booking it, 'all the interim is like a phantasma, or a hideous dream'. A decade or so ago, the entire exercise had been designed to test the patience of a saint. So, we ordinary mortals ended up with high blood pressure, palpitation, nervous tics and jumpiness; in other words, we became neurotic wrecks.

Just the act of getting through to the gas agency to book a fresh cylinder was fraught with suspense. I have even taken leave for that—desperate situations require desperate remedies. I knew the two numbers by memory and I would be glued to the telephone, making calls alternately to them, always hoping the perennially engaged numbers got disengaged at some point. They did, but that was in the hallowed lunch interval which was clearly sacrosanct for the employees, considering they would not even touch the telephones. Finally, I had no option but to go personally to the agency for the purpose. With the twenty-four hour automatic booking facility now available, at least the first part is easy.

But after the booking, the second stage—the guessing game—begins. When will the cylinder come home? The automatic booking system has its merits, but it's a clever system, for you can't clear doubts or ask questions to a machine. You wait on tenterhooks for the SMS informing you your cash memo is ready and the cylinder will be delivered shortly.

Shortly—that's the key word. How many days is 'shortly'? Your guess is as good as mine, but no one wishes to take a chance. Short of laying the red carpet to welcome the delivery man, all arrangements are made to receive him any time he condescends to stride in regally, the sceptre in the form of the cylinder balanced on his shoulder.

'Someone should be in the house when the gas man arrives,' is the golden rule around which every activity is planned. Recently we waited two days for the cylinder, taking turns even to go to the bathroom. I also had the money ready in my hand. When the power failed once, I kept the front door open and planted myself on the settee, eyes fixed unblinkingly on the gate and ears peeled for the sound of the delivery vehicle clanking to a stop. But it was like waiting for Godot; nothing happened, nobody came.

On the third morning, the doorbell finally rang, not in the strident, impatient manner that is the signature tune of the gas delivery man, but hesitantly. Maybe it's a new, more polite person, I thought. The seedy-looking chap who stood on the doorstep gave a wan smile. 'I need five hundred rupees for a heart operation,' he said, looking significantly at the notes in my hand. I recoiled. I could smell alcohol on his breath. 'Sir is not here and there's no money,' I said, blatantly painting my generous husband a tight-fisted scrooge. 'My family's going hungry without money,' he persisted. 'So is mine,' I retorted, 'without gas.' 'Oh, gas! That's for the gas? You won't get it now; they're all on strike. Give me a hundred, or a fifty. Even twenty would do.' I got rid of him with ten, shocked with the news about the strike.

I immediately rushed to the gas agency and joined the queue. I heard a man hurl abuse at the girls at the counter while another resorted to threats, a third wanted to see the elusive manager immediately. The girls listened with deadpan expressions, on occasion exchanging quick, amused glances. When it was my turn one girl said my booking had been cancelled for no one was at home when the cylinder was brought.

I couldn't believe my ears. 'Someone was there every second,' I protested and added, 'Casabianca is my middle name.' Unimpressed she continued, 'It's been re-booked and you'll get it shortly.'

I'm still waiting...

OF CREATURES GREAT AND SMALL

It's a Dog's Life, Anyway

I LIKE DOGS... FROM A DISTANCE. THE GREATER THE DISTANCE, the more amicably disposed I am towards them. I have nothing against dogs, man's best friends and all that, but I wish they'd leave me alone. Just one harrowing, high voltage chase by a mongrel in your childhood is enough to put the fear of the dog in you forever. My wary attitude stems from such an experience during my school days.

The canine in question was an old, weather-beaten, mangy stray; a comatose quadruped that doubled as a dog. Hardly anyone deigned to throw a cursory glance at it and it returned the compliment by royally ignoring everybody, preferring instead to sleep away its time in the lane I regularly took to school. It looked incapable of chasing the fleas and flies that worried it. Was the poor harmless thing even breathing, I occasionally wondered, until one day it proved unequivocally that it could not only breathe, but also growl and move—the day when, without any warning, it came to pulsating life with a sniff, a snarl and a spring in my direction.

Who would have thought the dog to have had so much energy in it? One minute it was dead to the world, the next it seemed to have only murder on its mind. Believe me, I had done nothing to provoke it—hadn't prodded it or yelled in its ear or stepped on its tail; I wish I had. The lane which had steps at regular intervals instantaneously became a level race track as my feet flew over it, stopping only when a quick glance over my shoulder showed that the quirky creature had resumed its old familiar torpid position. But if it could spring a surprise on me and act clever, I was cleverer; I changed my route.

Since then I have been very circumspect in my dealings with dogs. But they keep popping up everywhere and I have to find ways and means of dodging them. Not easy at all. I've noticed their owners are baffled that the whole world doesn't love their dogs with a fervour equalling their own. Try telling a dog lover, when you visit her house, you have mild cynophobia, which, by the way, means fear of dogs, and chances are she will look blank. She has never heard the word; the very idea that anyone could be afraid of dogs is alien to her. If you're lucky, she might look alarmed and reply, 'Sign of what? An infectious disease? Oh no, my precious poppet could catch it. Let me take him to another room.' Ah, but this is only wishful thinking.

What actually happens is that before even a bleat can escape my lips, the dog gambols towards me. But the owner only gazes indulgently at the canine apple of her eye and says, 'Haha, he won't do anything.' Not to you, but certainly to me, I think, as, my heart banging against my teeth, I leap for cover and try to hide behind whoever is near me.

Yes, for the dog lover, the dog greeting me with a bark loud enough to rip my head off, jumping on me and doing a war dance around me, sniffing suspiciously about my feet before licking them and baring its fangs ferociously as a preliminary to sinking them into some part of me, is nothing.

'He's just being playful,' she says, enjoying the fun. Or, 'See, he really likes you, that's why he's circling you. He doesn't do this to everybody.' So I have been singled out for the honour of suffering a silent heart attack. If I finally whisper in desperation that it be tied up, she reacts as if I have suggested inflicting the third degree on it. And gets offended that I referred to the dog as 'it' instead of 'he'.

A brisk evening walk is made brisker by the stray dogs that litter the pavements. I feel like an undercover agent as I dodge, duck, swerve, jump, cross and re-cross the road to avoid stepping on them or their poo.

The only time I ever got the better of them was when I once found myself playing Pied Piper to an assorted group. I quickly realised it wasn't me but the meat cutlets in my carry bag they were after. I furtively made a ball of the paper covering the cutlets and flinging it at them, dashed into my house. Every dog does not always have its, sorry, his or her day.

Gazing at Fish

GAZING AT FISH IN AN AQUARIUM IS VERY SOOTHING FOR your nerves, they say. It brings down your blood pressure, reduces levels of anxiety and creates a feeling of serenity. I wouldn't know, for I can never see the fish that live in the small aquarium in our dining room; I wouldn't even know if they're living at all. In fact, trying to catch a glimpse of the fish through the aquarium's moss-covered glass sides is enough to raise your stress levels, for they live in the strictest possible privacy with algae to the right of them, algae to the left of them, algae in front of them and algae all around them. It's not even a game of hide and seek they play with you; it is blind man's buff.

My husband prefers it that way. He says they are best left to themselves. 'Why do you want to soothe your nerves by looking at the fish? How can you be sure their anxiety levels don't rise when they look at you? Do you know that fish get stressed out too, and lose colour when that happens? We don't want pale, jittery fish in our tank. Let them live happily in their own world.'

He's in charge of the aquarium and after setting it up with great care he has, more or less, passed on the responsibility to nature. It's a great big secret now, obscured successfully by algae, but there is actually sand and gravel at the bottom of the tank, and there are shells too. A minute investigation might reveal small rocks and smooth stones arranged in the corners to form caves for the fish to play peek-a-boo. We had had fun finding the right plants and finally buying the fish. We had jumped at water wisteria and Java fern and Amazon something or the other when the pet shop assistant said these water plants needed only minimal maintenance. He warned us against vallisneria because fish sometimes ate it. We promptly purchased it. What if we forgot to feed the fish?

We were cautioned about introducing different varieties of fish into the tank. Certain fish just don't thrive in the company of certain others; so we decided to play safe by going for just guppies. It turns out, there's nothing guppies are more passionate about than one another's company. They began multiplying like mad, as if they had been set a deadline to populate the aquarium.

Now that the water seemed to be okay for the fish, we transferred almost all the guppies to the pond outside and decided to experiment with other varieties. Going by names, we introduced gentle varieties like angel fish, widow tetra and a solitary goldfish. They became great friends. Getting bolder, we introduced the beautiful fighter fish which, however, appeared quite tame.

As time passed, the novelty faded, our interest waned and the aquarium got shrouded with moss and algae. A friend who dropped by was curious about why the tank was so dark and murky. My husband began a lecture. 'Fish don't like light and need to sleep too. It's healthy for the fish to live in sombre, shadowy environs, with an aura of mystery....'

'But this looks like a murder mystery!' The friend exclaimed, cutting him short. She had spied a dead fish floating in a corner.

That shocked us. My husband peered into the tank and asked me accusingly, 'What's this floating here?'

'What's what floating where?' I countered, playing for time.

'This thing. What did you put in?'

'A bit of dosa,' I confessed. 'I thought it would be very nourishing.'

That was it. He took complete control of the aquarium. But the next day another fish was found dead. So it wasn't the dosa. I was relieved to be absolved of the crime. Could it be the fighter fish, finally playing true to its name? We isolated it. But the plot thickened. The deaths continued and we kept removing one fish after another and finally discovered the culprit when my husband's finger accidentally went too deep into the water and something gave it an eager, carnivorous jab. It was the docile angel, grown large on the meat of its fellows, and now biting the hand that fed it.

After that we've never had more than two or three fish at a time. My husband continues to show his love for them by keeping them well hidden in the dark, cool waters.

As for me, I love fish too. On my plate, that is.

Cat-astrophe

A LOT OF NOISE IS MADE ABOUT THE STRAY DOG MENACE, but when it comes to stray cats, it is they who make all the noise. Ask unfortunate residents of areas where cats regularly hold musical concerts at odd hours and watch them froth at the mouth as they recollect the caterwauling that keeps them awake all night. There isn't much of the gentle purring and meowing you associate with cats here; it is a cacophonous combination of growls, snarls, hisses and plaintive calls that starts from deep down their throats, rising to an ear splitting crescendo composed specifically to take your head apart.

But doubtless there's something special about cats. After reading my thoughts on canines, a student asked, 'Why dogs? They are so boring and predictable.' Ah, clearly she hadn't been chased by one. 'Cats are way cooler and more mysterious,' she asserted. Well, she's bang on there. Even a dyed-in-the-wool dog lover would be forced to admit that when it comes to style and dignity, the cat will win paws down.

I've had cats. In the house, I mean. Quite a variety, and each was a stray that walked into the house and didn't walk out. The first feline visitor went on a self-conducted tour with its nose in the air and soon curled up in a corner. I smelt a rat. Quite likely it did too, for it decided to stay put. My husband and my son, cat lovers both, were delighted by these encroachers-turned-denizens.

The pattern for looking after them was set with the first resident cat and never changed thereafter. It was based purely on the principle of division of labour. My husband and my son took care of its emotional needs—petting it, stroking its head, tickling its neck and tummy, saying sweet nothings to it in a language that neither they nor the cat understood but which gave deep satisfaction to all concerned, and of course lifting it onto their laps where it would promptly go to sleep.

I was assigned the job of feeding it and brushing its hair off cushions, bedspreads, rugs and wherever it chose to sleep, which was everywhere and all the time. Ogden Nash, the American humorist, said, 'The trouble with a kitten is that eventually it becomes a cat.' I beg to differ, for the best things about a cat are its toilet manners, its love for the great outdoors, its habit of burying its poo, all of which a kitten needs to learn. All strays that took up residence here were females and flirtatious to boot, keeping my hands full.

The other day, quite out of the blue, a friend asked, 'How do you get rid of a cat?' I was taken aback. Was she writing a murder mystery or did she want a solution to a practical problem? We've had about six cats so far, and all except one had died—some of old age, some of disease. Whenever one cat died, another would arrive, with uncanny timing, to take its place.

The last cat we had, was a small-built stray that came meowing in one rainy evening. It looked sick but quickly got better and began, to our great delight, to target lizards. One day it took ill. Too much gorging on lizards, likely. The vet we consulted prescribed some medicines and antibiotics. Use antibiotic eye drops, he said. That'd be swift and effective. He didn't know how prophetic his words were.

My son held the cat firmly in his grasp. When my husband tipped its head up, I handed him the drops and he swiftly put the required number in one eye. But before he could drop them into the other, the cat that had been lying motionless got miraculously energised and tearing itself free from my son's hands with a terrified yowl, shot out of the room, out of the house, out of the compound and into the wide open spaces.

It never came back. We hunted high and low. We heard it had been spotted at a very busy junction close by; it had been spied on top of a three storied building, seen near the railway station.... We wondered if it was contemplating suicide. But obviously, it not only survived, but passed the word round. Since then, though some make faces at us and mew expletives as they run along the wall, not one cat has walked in.

I told my friend, 'Try antibiotic eye drops.'

Termite Alert!

IRONY IS WHEN YOU WRITE A SHORT STORY ABOUT TERMITES only to discover that the malicious creatures have devoured the very pages of the magazine in which it had appeared. It was almost as if they had read the story and decided to finish it off by chewing and digesting it. They hadn't left a word behind. A good meal for them and heartbreak for me, for that was the only copy I had.

I discovered this last week when I lifted an old toffee tin one morning, only to find it come away in my hand with a good chunk of what remained of the shelf's wood stuck to its bottom. Along with some telltale white ants. Termite alert!!

This is literally an occupational hazard—an incident waiting to happen when you occupy an old house. I am attached to my home, but so, it appears, are the termites.

I frantically cleared the contents of the cupboard that included a pile of precious magazines and found, to my horror, that the termites had already destroyed the oldest issues at the bottom of the pile, and were now steadily working their way up. Some adventurous ones had begun to sink their teeth gleefully into other books too when I discovered them and applied the brakes on their greedy feasting.

I needed consolation. My husband was away, so I told my friend that termites had got into my books. 'Move,' she said. Move? The books or the termites, I asked. 'You,' she replied. 'I mean, it's time for you to move house. Do you know,' she continued dreamily, 'I've always considered unleashing termites the most effective method for landlords to evict tenants who dig their feet in and refuse to budge. But of course, the method needs the active cooperation of armies of termites.'

What nonsense! I was quite indignant. Here I was hoping for sympathy and some practical advice on how to get rid of the pests, and she rambles on about using termites to get rid of troublesome tenants. Disheartened, I went back to clearing the remains of the siege. The only good, if you can call it that, was the termites had also destroyed a lot of supposed junk I had been disinclined to get rid of, leaving me with no choice but Hobson's—of burning the remnants.

What temporary method of damage control could I adopt? I thought hard, and cleverly decided to buy naphthalene balls. If they can repel ants, I thought, they could extend the courtesy to white ants too. I bought a dozen packets and strewed the naphthalene balls here, there and everywhere.

A late brainwave prompted me to go to the internet for information. 'Termite colonies are decentralised, spaghetti-like things that can range from 10,000 insects to half a million...'—frightening numbers, those—'...and could have reached over from your neighbour's yard a half-acre away.' Oops, that's taking the 'love thy neighbour' commandment too far.

'Do not panic if there is termite activity,' advised a wise guy. 'Too late,' I confided to my computer screen, 'that was the first thing I did.' But the panic stage was now over. No one is immune to termite attacks, I was told next. Even the White House and the Statue of Liberty have had to deal with termites. Well, that's some relief. I'm glad the little fellas are so egalitarian, but I still can't bring myself to love them.

The next suggestion pushed me to try beneficial nematodes. Beneficial what? I skipped that and went to the next. Expose your wood to sunlight. Thank you very much, but it's raining heavily. 'If you are in a rainy area,'—aha, now you're talking—'... freeze the termites.' What?? Place my furniture in a freezer? Think I'm living in a doll's house? You must be crazy! 'Use boric acid.' At last, a sensible and intelligible suggestion. I decided to get it after my husband returned. Anyway, I had already used naphthalene balls as a short term precautionary measure.

I decided to check the net for confirmation that my decision had indeed been clever. And what did I find? The startling information that termites actually produce naphthalene and use it to defend themselves from their natural enemies like ants, fungi and nematode worms. Yes, remember the beneficial nematodes? Well, apparently they are worms that can kill termites. I was glad to add to my general knowledge, but dumbfounded to discover I had actually been helping the termites by supplying them with naphthalene! Irony again. I've still not recovered all the naphthalene balls I had generously flung around...

ON THE MOVE

A Pony Ride

AN UNUSUAL CLIP-CLOP SOUND CAPTURED MY ATTENTION while on my walk last week. I turned to see a horse trotting merrily along. The rider on the makeshift saddle basked in the admiring looks he received. Riding looks so deceptively simple, I thought wistfully, and couldn't help recalling my first and only equestrian experience many years back.

I was in Ooty with my final year BA students. While the other teacher and I were busy with some formalities, several girls took sedate rides on a miserable, skin-and-bones pony that looked sad, sleepy and bored at the same time. A bunch of timid girls standing around told me they were scared of horses.

'Call that a horse?' I commented. 'That poor thing appears more scared of you. What's to fear in a slow pony ride when the keeper holds the reins and strolls beside it? Come on girls, don't fuss so.'

'Why don't you take a ride then, Ma'am?' a girl, whose name I don't recollect, but with whom I have a score to settle, suggested playfully. The others took up the chant, 'Ma'am is next! Ma'am, go on a ride!' The pony's keeper decided to join the hullabaloo and said, 'Ma'am next! Ma'am ke liye free!' The other teacher smartly pushed me towards the pony and disappeared from the horizon.

My light-hearted words of encouragement to the lily-livered group of girls had backfired. I muttered words of protest. I feebly said I'd never been on a pony before except to have a photograph taken on the clay model of a pink horror when I was three but no one listened. By this time, all the girls had formed an excited group and some interested passers-by, sensing fun for free, quite like my ride, joined them. I gave in.

The keeper tossed me up and the girls flocked around, some making sure I was seated properly, some thrusting the reins into my hands, others pushing my feet into the stirrups, all the time filling my ears with encouraging words.

'The round's over in no time, Ma'am.'

'The pony's dreadfully slow, Ma'am, it's hardly a ride!'

One girl peered close and asked, 'Ma'am, are you scared? You look a strange, chalky brown.'

'That's just my natural colour, child,' I whispered, smiling wanly and trying to hide the trembling of my lips.

The keeper added in a reassuring tone, 'I'll hold one end of the reins and run alongside, nothing to fear. Move away, girls! Huah! Huah!' He slapped the pony on its side and the pony, rudely woken from its somnambulism, gave one startled leap and took off at a gallop. I held on to the reins for dear life and closed my eyes. I was vaguely aware of joyful yells, shouts and delighted applause coming from a great distance, but was completely preoccupied with keeping my balance and staying on the pony.

Movies like *Sholay* had conned me into imagining that riding was the easiest thing on earth. Who would have thought sitting on a pony would be like sitting on a bag loosely filled with bones! It was a rude, literally bone-shaking, awakening. Just when I'd hold my place, by locating a bone under me, it would shift its position for no rhyme or reason leaving me twirling on emptiness. Panicking, I'd do a desperate twist, turn and waggle in an effort to perch on something solid.

Not only could I count the pony's bones, I became aware of mine too. Tossed this way and that, I raced along like John Gilpin. When I finally gained close to the cheers, I opened my eyes with relief believing the ride was over. But the devil had entered the keeper who gave the pony more slaps, clicked his tongue, mouthed more huah, huahs and we raced away on two more crazy rounds.

When the pony finally slowed down I was sprawled all over it, my eyes shut and my arms locked in a tight embrace around its neck as if I couldn't bear to part with it.

'Ma'am, ride over,' the keeper shouted into my ears. Wild cheering greeted me when I opened my eyes and was helped off the dreadful creature that looked balefully at me.

'Great riding, Ma'am!' exclaimed a girl. 'Lucky you! You got three rides! What speed!'

'Ma'am enjoyed the ride,' announced the sadistic keeper. 'Want another?' he asked maliciously, with half a wink.

I was too busy putting my body and soul together to reply.

Hips or Chips?

'HOT HIPS SOLD HERE,' DECLARED A BOARD IN FRONT OF A shop. 'Goodness, how brazen can you get!' I exclaimed, instinctively pulling my saree pallu closer about me. Had I read correctly? I wore my glasses and took a closer look. Yes, I wasn't mistaken but could now see that a naughty hand had chipped off the 'C' from 'Chips.' I'm no authority on Kerala hips but as far as chips are concerned, they are easily the best.

My husband is always amazed at the enthusiasm with which my sisters cart kilos of banana chips whenever they come down for a visit. Their mode of travel is never any deterrent in their desire to haul them to Chennai, Bangalore, Dubai or the US. International flights bearing tasty banana and jackfruit chips have crossed seas while trains and inter-state buses have lugged the delicious freight uncomplainingly. It's this overwhelming devotion to chips and bananas that had landed me in trouble a few years back.

I was in Chennai for a family wedding and about to leave for the airport to head back to Thiruvananthapuram when one of my sisters brought me some luscious-looking mangoes. 'Mangoes,' she gushed. 'From our own trees. Organic, and taste like heaven.'

'I can't take them,' I objected. 'My suitcase's already overflowing and I can't carry them in my handbag.'

Someone produced a jute textile bag and before I knew what was happening, another sister nonchalantly pulled out some clothes from a plastic cover in my suitcase and shoved them into the bag, brushing aside my protests that I had kept them separately for they were to be laundered. 'That's perfect. They will cushion the mangoes and a stain here or there won't matter,' she said. 'And take this small bag of rice too. From our own fields. Organic. Smell it. Heavenly.' She thrust a handful of rice under my nose and a grain travelled up my nostril setting me sneezing like crazy.

With watery eyes, I watched my sisters enthusiastically fill the bag. They live by the principle that there is no room for empty space in any form of luggage. Raw groundnuts, fresh vegetables, sugarcane, palm sprouts and lentils found their way in. Feeling the bag and finding a pocket of air along one side, a sister nudged in a diary and a banana stand.

'Is that allowed as hand baggage?' I asked, scrutinising the shapeless thing in dismay. I had hardly ever travelled by air and believed one should take decent-looking bags. 'It looks uncouth.'

'Nonsense!' A sister looked disapprovingly at me. 'Don't be so squeamish,' said another. 'See, it's respectable now. Quite "couth"!' She laughed and shielding the contents with a magazine, used a handkerchief to tie the wooden handles securely together in a butterfly knot. I sighed and left for the airport with the heavenly cargo. You can't argue with older sisters.

With the bag placed unobtrusively at the carry-on baggage security check, I went for the passenger screening and returned to find it in the eye of a storm. 'Isn't that yours?' asked a security personnel, drawing everyone's attention to my bulging textile bag that suddenly seemed to dwarf everything else around. A crowd quickly collected, gazing at the bag as children would a performing monkey. I hung my head and nodded mutely, waiting for him to declare such bags unacceptable; instead he announced, 'There's something suspicious in it.'

'What?' I looked up, shocked. 'Yes.' He had, apparently, run the bag over the screening check three times and all three times it had set off a telltale beep. 'We have to examine the contents.' He untied the hanky, flung aside the magazine and dug in. Out came a shabby housecoat, followed by an underskirt. Someone laughed. What next? A fashionable lady sniggered. He hesitated, then curtly signalled that I take over.

I unearthed mangoes, rice, lentils and sugarcane. Groundnuts, more clothes, vegetables, palm sprouts and a towel followed, in that order, with the diary and the banana stand emerging last. The man was puzzled. He turned the bag upside down. A tomato fell and burst on his shoe.

Annoyed, he flicked through the diary while someone unfolded the flat banana stand into its L shape. On the perpendicular board was a tiny metal hook. 'At last! The culprit!' The man was ecstatic, then frowned, 'What is it, anyway?'

'A banana holder. The hook's to hang a bunch of bananas. They can be made into banana chips.' I explained.

He looked at me as if I had gone bananas and snapped, 'What silly inventions! Wasting our time.' The crowd melted away, disappointed, and as I thrust everything higgledy-piggledy into my bag, the fashionable lady drawled, 'Can't you just buy hot chips instead?' And sashayed away, swaying her hips.

Chasing the Parcel

'IS YOUR NAME KRRR...ERR...UM...SA?' A VOICE GRATED ON THE landline. 'Not yet that,' I said. He was from a courier service, he explained, and probably wanted to make sure people with such unpronounceable names did exist. He had a parcel to deliver. A parcel? Nobody had intimated me about it and I couldn't recall having ordered anything either. A surprise gift? I was filled with a warm glow of affection for that generous and thoughtful sender.

I volunteered the correct pronunciation and when I had surpassed myself with excellent directions that would have brought the most geographically challenged person to my house blindfolded, he asked if I could collect the parcel from the office.

Well, really! I reminded him my house was very close to the courier office, adding I was too ill to go around collecting parcels. My voice, with significant help from a sore throat, was hoarse anyway, and I coughed for that authentic effect. He said he'd bring it and disappeared from my life.

That was on a Friday. I waited in anticipation, but nobody came. The parcel didn't appear on Saturday either or the Monday after. Now, I began to obsess over the parcel. 'Where's that guy?' I asked my husband, peeved. I hadn't stepped out of the house since that historic phone call.

'Maybe the gas delivery man is now working for the courier service,' my husband suggested, eyes twinkling. 'That could explain the suspense, drama and mystery.'

On Tuesday, I began my investigation. Unfortunately, the courier chap had called on the landline and with no caller ID facility, I had to hunt for the phone number. After some effort, I got a number that was continuously busy and when I finally got through, a brusque voice gave me another number the moment I began narrating my story. One number led to another, after long delays of busy tones or unanswered calls, and thus, passed from telephonic pillar to post, I was led a merry dance, every call leading nowhere.

At last a man–I thought he was a kind soul, alas!–listened to my grievance and asked for the tracking number. That stumped me and I confessed I didn't know who had sent the parcel. He perked up. 'Then we are helpless.'

'Can't you use my name to track?' I asked.

'Can't.' He sounded pleased and added, 'Why didn't you ask that man for more details?' Lesson learnt. 'But when someone asks for directions to deliver a parcel, you don't cross-examine him,' I countered.

'You should. Find the tracking number.' He cut the call with this jaunty advice.

My husband asked me to forget it, certain it was some useless free gift for a magazine subscription that was better off touring the country than cluttering the house. But I wasn't giving up. I called a friend who sends the occasional surprise gift and felt quite foolish when she laughingly asked if I was giving her a broad hint.

The next day, I headed to the main office where my story was greeted with indifference. I stood my ground. Eventually I was led upstairs to a lady seated before a computer, a phone stuck on her right ear, eyes on the monitor, fingers flying over the keyboard. She listened to me while talking on the phone, simultaneously giving directions to a chap who had materialised before her. I realised she was addressing me when she chanted the 'tracking number' mantra for a bit. I stuck to my theme of 'the name, do a search with that.' After ages, she said my parcel had come again.

Again? What did that mean? She claimed nobody was home the first time it had been sent out and it had been returned. The sender had forwarded it a second time.

'Oh, okay,' I said, sounding uncertain. 'But why didn't that guy bring it on Friday?' She shrugged her left shoulder and lost interest in me. That evening my husband went to the courier office that delivers to our area and drew a blank. 'Name's no use. Tracking number, tracking number,' the lady there had parroted.

Why don't courier services follow the sensible practice of the good old postal department of leaving behind intimation if the door is locked? Whoever said privatisation was the panacea for all our woes has not experienced privatised inefficiency and indifference. Add rudeness to the delectable mix and you have an excellent recipe for frustration.

Now I'm on track. I've discovered the sender and have the tracking number. Nothing more to be done. I'm waiting for the call, 'Is your name Keer … na…sa?'

'Booking' a Seat

WHO SAID YOU NEED SMART PHONES TO BOOK SEATS ON trains and buses? All you require is a handkerchief, and the grimier, the better.

The other day the train had barely pulled into a station when a large, hairy, male hand plunged in through the window, startling the bespectacled young man huddled in the side seat out of his catnap. It dangled a tiny lady's handkerchief like a pendulum under his nose. Now fully awake, the chap, showing signs of being a hypochondriac, involuntarily jerked his head away, stopped breathing and watched the grubby hanky anxiously while trying to distance himself from it and the germs it probably carried. But the hanky persisted in pursuing his nose.

Alarmed, he withdrew further and further into his seat quite determined to disappear through its back, when the fierce-looking owner of the hairy hand peered in. 'There!' With an outward thrust of his chin, he indicated a spot just vacated by a passenger on the seat of the sleeper coach. 'This!' he commanded, offering the hanky as if it were a sweet-smelling bouquet.

Overawed, the youth obeyed the monosyllabic orders, held the hanky with the tips of his fingers and dropped it on the seat almost as gracefully as would a lady from medieval Europe who wished to show favour to her chosen knight.

He was just in time. An army of passengers swarmed in. The first thing they noticed as their darting eyes searched for a perch was the hanky occupying a seat, but they didn't take it amiss. Such is the sanctity of a handkerchief when used to indicate a 'booked' seat that no one dared pick it up or shove it aside. Instead, following the policy of the proverbial camel in the tent, they seated themselves about it, shrinking the space where it rested. Viewing the drama from the seat opposite, I thought only a tiny Thumbelina could fit herself in the space that remained.

How wrong I was! A lady of generous proportions hustled in, scattering all who stood in her way with great authority before claiming the hanky and the seat. Obviously an old hand at this, she blew her nose to establish ownership of her handkerchief, then marked her territory by wriggling expertly into the space, miraculously getting it to expand. It is an art and she did it exceptionally well.

In no time, her family, including the hairy-handed spouse was seated around her and, for good measure, she accommodated a couple of kids on her capacious lap. I could only watch with admiration.

It is a long established practice to book seats this way in buses. People fling bags, handkerchiefs, towels or magazines through the windows on their chosen seats or any available seat to book them. It's almost a Frisbee-throwing match out there with passengers exhibiting enviable aim and precision to land these identified flying objects with great expertise on the chosen targets. This is where Sports Authority representatives should gather to spot talent.

Generally, nobody disputes their claims, but on occasion some not-so-conscientious objector performs the sacrilegious act of removing the marker to sit on the seat. My husband said he once saw a man do that and when the belligerent claimant arrived, he nonchalantly handed the hanky over. Very quickly battle lines were drawn and the whole bus got involved in an exciting free for all.

Hankies, along with the ubiquitous towel, are also used to mark the attendance of a person. I remember going with my friend to an office and being confronted by a vacant chair at the relevant section. 'He's present,' the person at the next table said, pointing to a towel draped neatly over the back of the chair. 'He's gone for tea, but will be back.'

We waited and waited, then returned the next day to get the same response, only this time, the towel was over the armrest and he had gone for an early lunch. More visits followed and it became a game for us to guess where the towel would be and where the owner would have gone. My friend wondered if the towel was an example of synecdoche, a figure of speech in which a part is made to represent a whole, or metonymy, where a word or a phrase is used to stand in for another word. I said I wasn't sure about that, but it definitely meant the person was not in his seat.

One fine day, when we reached the office as usual, there was empty space where the chair had once stood. Synecdoche? Metonymy? All I knew was that the little hope the towel's presence had provided was now gone.

No Directions, Please

I HEARD SOMEONE OBSERVE THE OTHER DAY THAT MEN HAVE drive but no direction. I would like to alter that to 'men can drive but won't ask for directions.' This is strictly based on home experience, but my friends assure me their spouses are no different. Obviously it is a male characteristic, one that gave rise to the tongue-in-cheek story about Moses spending forty years in the wilderness because he wouldn't ask for directions.

My husband and my son have an excellent memory for places and know most of the lanes and roads of the city, even the ones I had no idea existed; hence their faith in reaching any place without help. For my husband, locating an unheard of place is a challenge and he doesn't mind going round and round in circles till he finds it, though even he finds his patience tested when he gets vague directions. He continues doggedly while delivering mini lectures under his breath about parking problems, driving constraints at peak hours and how bad people, especially women, are at giving directions.

Indeed, we women are often guilty of this charge, probably because many of us don't drive, but some instructions can drive you up the wall: 'Go to the junction, turn right, go straight, again go straight, you'll find some shops there. Turn and go straight left. My house is in that lane. Sometimes you might find a stray dog or two outside the gate.' Such inept hints stump my husband, but then he loves a challenge and vacuous directions strengthen his resolve to successfully find the place against these steep odds.

I can't drive, but I'm a master at asking for directions when I'm on my own. Being geographically challenged, as my husband puts it, asking for directions is the only way for me. In fact, I leave a trail of vague, assorted questions behind when I, willy-nilly, reach my destination.

I remember the first time I ventured to Kariavattom University campus by myself.

My husband dropped me at Thampanoor bus terminus, at the exact spot where buses taking that route start their journey. One couldn't go wrong from there—or so he thought. Clearly, he hadn't reckoned with my special inabilities. A bus pulled in and I nervously asked the bus conductor who popped out like a jack-in-the-box if it would go to Kariavattom University campus. I was specifically tutored to add 'university campus' when I got my ticket.

He nodded. Beginner's luck, I told myself, thrilled, and selected a comfortable window seat. I love window seats. But soon it struck me I was the only passenger. A rickety old woman, after hard-selling me some green, sour oranges, laughed like a hyena and said the bus wouldn't leave till kingdom come.

So much for beginner's luck. I got down and asked a plump lady standing nearby which bus would go to Kariavattom University campus. She pointed to one that was filling up. Relieved, I joined the crowd that absorbed me in its midst and shoved me in. Soon, the bus started. Walking expertly inside the moving vehicle, the conductor approached me for the fare. 'No, no,' he snapped when I told him. 'This won't stop at the university campus.' 'But...but... I was told it goes there,' I stammered. 'It goes there all right, but doesn't stop there. Can't you read the bus board? This is a fast passenger bus. Now get off.' He rang the bell muttering something about illiterate people wasting his time.

Another ten minutes were spent asking for directions to the particular terminal before I found my way back to it. I wasn't taking any more chances. Soon, everybody around knew where I was headed. They entered into the spirit of things and there was much bonhomie as they directed me to the right bus, but for good measure I went around to ask the driver before clambering in. In those crucial few minutes the bus got crowded and I was propelled to the front. I implored the conductor, and whoever would listen, to let me know when the bus reached my destination.

Soon I got a seat at the back, where once again I made my entreaties. 'Next stop, university campus,' the conductor announced. I jumped up and clung to the metal post near the door, swaying to the rhythm of the bus's movement, all set to alight at the right moment. When the bus drew to a halt, everyone, from the driver to a cheeky boy in front, twirled their necks like robots obeying a command and yelled in a delighted chorus, 'Kariavattom University campus!'

That's how easy it is to reach an unfamiliar place if you only ask for directions.

HOME AFFAIRS

Not Floored

A VISITOR WHO CAME HOME THE OTHER DAY KEPT HER head bowed for a long time. Reverentially, I thought, impressed with the deep respect she was showing us. After a good few minutes, she jerked her head up and exclaimed, 'Your floor's mosaic!' Aha! So that was what she had been doing—scanning my floor minutely. She had been floored by my floor. I was delighted. Here at last was a connoisseur of flooring, a rare species.

'Yes,' I nodded like a bobblehead doll. I was convinced that appreciative comments about my beautiful floor were hovering on her lips; paeans of praise were about to be sung. I prepared to accept them graciously. But I was hopelessly off target. 'Nobody has mosaic floors anymore,' were the sanctimonious words that followed, uttered with the faintest hint of a sneer in her voice.

'But you just said *my* floor was mosaic,' I said, quick to pounce on the logical flaw in the argument. Not one to be deterred, she said she meant hardly any houses had mosaic floors.

'Mosaic is passé,' she said in a blasé tone. Turning her nose just a little in the air, she continued, 'And it looks like it's not even been polished lately.' Ouch! She was right. On both counts. My floor's common grey, black and white pockmark-like patterned mosaic is distinctly out of favour with interior decorators and has been so for many years now. That's also why the floor hasn't been polished—the polishing experts, along with the floors, had disappeared without a trace.

Floors have come a long way from the simple and the functional to the ornate and extravagant. The intrusion of 'lookism' into the construction industry has led to highly polished and expensive floor tiles taking over from what Laurie Baker, the architect after nature's own heart, had advocated — humble but sensible floors made of mud and smeared with cow dung, or made from rough stone, cement or terracotta...

From stone to mosaic floor tiles was just a short, although expensive, step. Variety began to flourish right under people's feet as glazed ceramic decorative tiles, marble, polished granite and travertine tiles begged to be trod upon. The classy vitrified tiles, so popular now, have left careless walkers petrified and heavily bandaged; they are without doubt an orthopaedist's dream.

I told our guest I liked my old-fashioned unpolished mosaic; it wasn't slippery and its design camouflaged the dust on it—two excellent reasons to retain the floor in all its faded glory. But she appeared unconvinced and was clearly not done with me yet.

She lifted the curtain and scanned the garden. 'You don't believe in trimming plants, do you? Call that a garden? All overgrown and full of weeds!' The contemporary emphasis on the natural look, of allowing plants to grow higgledy-piggledy, suited my lazy approach to gardening perfectly. 'A garden should sustain nature, help the eco-system, and, to borrow from Wordsworth, be "green to the very door",' I responded, sounding like a textbook environmentalist. 'No manicured, pedicured lawns for me,' I added with a smile. Wasted words of wisdom, for she wasn't listening.

She continued, quite the lawn ranger, 'You've space for a lawn, but you let it go to seed. Just look at the grass!' Her reference to lawn, seed and grass reminded me of Wimbledon. 'For the cows,' I said, ridiculously. 'Remember, it's Wimbledon time.' I couldn't resist this non sequitur. She looked perplexed. I decided not to elaborate upon Ivan Lendl's famous 'Grass is for cows' excuse for not winning Wimbledon. 'Wimbledone? What's that? Who, anyway, is Wimble? And cows? You keep cows?' She sniffed delicately.

This was the time to tell her that the house right behind ours has a gobar gas plant. I sprang it on her and she promptly rose to her feet, breathing out all the time. Biogas plants don't smell, I tried to reassure her. Her one way breathing that sounded like an engine chugging out of the station made me anxious; I hoped she wouldn't faint on my ancient floor or in my weedy garden.

As she staggered out she noticed the pond, and remarked, 'Covered by moss! What's inside?' Crocodiles, sharks and some piranhas, I wanted to tell her, but decided to stick to the truth. 'Some guppies and more weeds. We found a snake in it too.'

That did it. She breathed out explosively as if she had applied the emergency brakes, and scooted. I have a feeling she might not visit again.

The Summer of Heat

'ANTS MEAN RAIN,' I ANNOUNCED, SWEAT TRICKLING LIKE rivulets down my face. 'I thought ants mean bites,' my husband laughed, looking pointedly at my left eyelid that had begun to swell, courtesy an ant bite. 'Maybe, but they mean rain too,' I responded, continuing to gaze squint-eyed at the rows of ants marching over the bedspread with the same joy that Wordsworth is supposed to have felt when he saw a rainbow in the sky.

Normally, ants—big, small, black, red, the biting kind or the harmless variety—evoke only one reaction in me: 'Get rid of them.' But this time, I was actually pleased, detecting in their presence a hint of approaching rains. For the city had never been so hot.

'The temperature is 38 degrees, 38! Can you beat it?' I remarked, watching the weather bulletin after de-anting the bedspread. As if on cue, the power failed and I got the full impact of the heat. I folded a newspaper supplement and fanned myself with it.

'Palakkad can,' replied my husband, who had worked there for a few years. 'Anyway, why all this fuss?' he asked, and remarked playfully that with one eye half shut, I bore a marked resemblance to the actress Lalita Pawar when she played the nasty mother-in-law in old Hindi films.

It's difficult to think up a spirited retort when your eye hurts and you are sweating like a pig. But I did manage to glare at him with one eye. 'Haha, now you look exactly like her,' he chortled before reverting to the topic of summer heat. 'Palakkad resembles a furnace in summer. But did we complain? Never. Because the Malayalee knows how to combat heat.'

And he sang the virtues of the cotton dhoti and the mundu. Sweating, he contended, is nature's way of cooling the body. 'And when it gets hot, remove the shirt. Simple. If it becomes too hot, remove the vest and what do you get? The air conditioned effect.' He demonstrated this. My husband seeks warmth with the enthusiasm of a sun-loving animal; it's the cold that he finds unbearable.

'Take a few extra baths,' he added. 'Sleep with the windows open in houses with wooden ceilings or thatched roofs, houses built in sylvan settings. Hey presto, the heat is overcome. We shall overcome, we shall overcome, we shall...'

'Wait a minute! You got the tense wrong,' I cut his refrain short. 'The Malayalee *knew* how to combat heat. Not anymore. Try asking an IT professional or a bank officer to wear a dhoti or mundu to office and do a strip tease when the temperature starts soaring. And all very well to talk about natural air conditioning, but spare a thought for women. Now don't start off about the enlightened Attingal maharani's attire when she received the British negotiators. That was long ago, before the British brought Victorian prudery with them and left it behind when they returned to England.'

To my great relief, power was restored and I took a casual look at the newspaper supplement that had been my temporary fan. It was a summer special, full of exciting possibilities for the season and cheerful suggestions on how to combat the heat. Recipes for a variety of refreshing drinks, ice creams in exciting flavours, exotic desserts and cool salads made it seem as if summer was a treat waiting to be experienced.

Sweat running down your face? Change the make-up. Sticky hair? Go for a smart bob. In the fashion section, models looked cool flaunting gorgeous cotton sarees and light, summery dresses in pastel shades. There were advertisements for air conditioners, fans, water coolers, trendy sunglasses and the right footwear. The tourism industry dangled the carrot of idyllic spots where a sweltering summer would be transformed into one long honeymoon.

Tell me another, I snorted, flinging the newspaper supplement away and running a hand through my sweaty hair. The truth about summer is intense heat, power failures, water shortage, dust, fatigue, profuse sweating, and summer special diseases. The mindless cutting of trees and the new apartment culture have made it worse. The only way to beat it is to complain and bear it.

'Drink lots of water, don't get dehydrated,' my husband offered yet another pearl of wisdom and took a deep swig. 'Aaaah!' he exclaimed.

'Yes, nothing like the satisfaction of drinking water,' I replied, nodding in approval.

'Satisfaction?' he spluttered. 'The water jug is full of ants.' I looked with some pleasure at his swelling lips and the hint of dark clouds in the horizon.

Fresh as Paint

THE OTHER DAY SOME PLASTER FELL LIKE CONFETTI FROM the ceiling of our drawing room, festooning my head with unerring precision. Your natural instinct when you are bombarded from above by alien objects is to identify the source. I looked up, a very foolish thing to do, as I discovered in hindsight, for I got the aftershock bang on my face and a tiny particle entered my eye. Never do this when a bird decides to practise target bombing on you either; the consequences are eye-popping, but that's another story.

After getting the mote out I pronounced, 'I knew this was coming. No plaster can remain impervious to all those loud guffaws yesterday when our friends came over. It's just delayed reaction.'

One of our friends had patented a uniquely explosive laughter that started in his belly, then rumbled its way up like an active volcano, gathering strength and momentum during its journey, to finally erupt in an uproarious blast that had the power to shatter glass window panes. We have strong iron grills in the front room—foresight here—leaving the ceiling to face the music.

'Rubbish!' my husband retorted. 'It is because of all that rainwater on the terrace. It's been raining the whole year and I've been expecting the ceiling to collapse on us any time.' I looked at him, surprised. Exaggeration is my department and if he resorts to it, it usually means something has really agitated him. 'No time to lose,' he exclaimed and rang up the contractor who reached the house even before the call was completed—he had apparently been waiting for the summons to take up from where he had left off ever since he had undertaken the painting of the gate and the compound wall a month back.

Now began the process that resembled the story of the camel getting his nose into the Arab's tent. Once the rusty ladder was discovered and cajoled into service, the contractor shimmied up for a close look. Identifying the problem, he shouted—'Clogged drain pipe, water retention, seepage, corrosion, weakening of the concrete. The terrace must be re-concreted. Leave it all to me.'

Sacks of cement arrived and migrant labourers too. In fact, we were woken up in the morning by the battering on the locked gate. It was the contractor, with the labourers in tow, one of whom was already removing his shirt in preparation of changing into his working gear even before the gate was opened. What zeal, I thought, suitably impressed by his work ethic.

The repair crew, bringing pandemonium in its wake, took over. There was hammering and scraping on the terrace punctuated with ear-splitting instructions from the overseer. After the debris was cleared, the re-laying of the terrace floor began—two coats of concrete and whatever, we were told, strong enough to withstand carpet-bombing. From that to painting the shabby terrace was a small step, and we agreed to the front of the house being painted too, the cementing having left rivulets of white running down the walls.

'What colour?' asked the contractor, eagerly pointing out hues of ghastly green, blue, pink and yellow on the shade card. 'The house should look nice and bright.' Unhappy with our sombre choice of black and white for the compound wall and grey for the gate, he hoped we would make amends for such aberrations.

'Grey,' we chorused, 'with a dark grey border.' He hid his disappointment with a sunny smile and responded gallantly, 'Smart colour!' His not to reason why, his but to smile and shrug it by. 'And the grills?' he continued, 'They are rusty.' Now putty in the hands of the contractor, my husband said with a sigh, 'Black and white.'

Later, when I went to examine how the work was progressing in the front of the house, I was treated to a scene that was right out of a circus—two legs belonging to an invisible man were dangling over the terrace, a very visible second person was acrobatically painting from an upside down position, a third was ballet dancing on the sill and a fourth was performing a delicate balancing act on a wobbling step ladder while cleaning the inner roof of the car shed.

From the front to the sides, and then to the back of the house was a natural progression. In no time, the painters were inside, painting the doors and windows. 'Green for the windows,' the contractor made a last ditch effort. 'White,' my husband declared, determined to show who was boss. The contractor smiled and asked, 'So, what about the roof of the bathroom outside? It's falling apart.'

The Elusive Newspaper

IN MY HOUSE, A SIMPLE TASK LIKE LOOKING FOR A NEWSPAPER becomes a job that could stump MI6. It could go just about anywhere and when you subscribe to three dailies, the confusion gets confounded threefold.

My sister-in-law wanted a newspaper, my husband said, and without waiting for further details, I immediately went to get all of them. They begin their day draped over the chairs in the front room. That's my husband's contribution to the room's decor. Every morning he religiously collects the papers that have been hurled over the gate by two energetic newspaper boys who, I strongly suspect, play Frisbee in their spare time. Both of them seem fuelled by the challenge of flinging the papers far and wide and each appears to be in competition with the other to toss them to the most inaccessible parts of the front yard.

My husband gets an impromptu quota of morning exercise when he bends down and sometimes, on all fours, stretches his hands to remote areas under the car where a paper lies hidden, often out-leaping the startled stray cat that shoots out like a missile after being rudely jolted out of its slumber by the infiltration of an alien arm into its adopted territory.

After these exhausting exertions, he carries his booty to the front room, distributes it over the furniture, gets back his breath, takes the nearest newspaper and disappears into the bathroom.

I took the newspapers in and then realised I hadn't asked the elementary questions crucial to the successful accomplishment of detective work involved in locating a missing newspaper—the name of the publication and the date. My husband gave the newspaper's name and a date from the previous week before doing a vanishing act. More assured now, I went to the papers stocked in a huge pile on a shelf in the dining room and began scanning them for the particular one. Things got interesting as I read juicy bits of gossip that had missed my eye earlier. I was still at it when my husband returned.

'Not found it yet?' he asked, joining in the search. The paper in question was soon declared missing. 'Where could it have gone?' my husband asked. 'We haven't sold the papers recently. Are you sure you haven't taken it to soak up the oil after frying pappadams?' I was certain I had not done that; I have special magazines for that purpose.

'Or maybe you've used it for making chapatis,' he suggested. That was a possibility. I generally place a newspaper under the rolling board to collect the flour that might fall when I spread the dough. That's when I come across more bits of interesting news. One gets to read newspapers in a variety of unconventional ways. Who hasn't come across juicy tidbits in newspapers wrapped around their roadside purchases? Or sensational news items in paper cones that they buy from peanut sellers?

I went to check and realised I had discarded the paper, after I had made chapatis, the previous day. I sifted through the dustbin and found that the paper I had thrown away, now full of ants, wasn't the right one either. I brushed off the ants, but a particularly painful bite reminded me that a few days back, I had spread an ant-infested newspaper under the hot sun on the terrace and forgotten about it. It had rained since and now I found the sheets lying scattered about, looking yellow, crumpled and woebegone. They had lost their identity but the date was faintly visible and I was grateful this soggy, camouflaged newspaper wasn't the right one.

Now I went to the one place I hadn't checked, my husband's bathroom where he has his 'loobrary', a collection of carefully selected books, magazines and papers that serve as reading material during time spent there. I didn't find the errant paper but I did locate, to my indignation, a half-read book I had been frantically hunting for. It didn't deserve to be there, I protested, while my husband delineated five good reasons why he believed it had found its rightful place.

While the debate continued, the abused book that I had placed on the bed slipped through the gap between the bed and the wall. Bending to retrieve it, I spied something white nestling against the wall. It was a newspaper, the elusive one we were looking for!

MISADVENTURES IN THE GARDEN

A Snake is a ... Snake

A SNAKE IS A SNAKE IS A SNAKE IS A SNAKE. AS A POETIC assertion, it's fine, but not when you find one inside the pond in your garden. 'There's a snake in our pond,' said my husband the other day as nonchalantly as one would say 'There's a crow on the tree.' 'Sssssssnake?' I hissed in alarm and jumped. But my jump was nothing compared with the jump Ajay, my son's friend, gave when he heard about the snake two days later. But then I'm jumping the gun here. Let me go back to the beginning.

My husband is a physisaphile. In case the word is Greek to you, it is...er... Greek for one who loves plants and animals. A snake for him is just a snake, a creature of nature. If the one in the pond had lost its way and fallen in, it was more to be pitied than censured. Not so for me. The primeval fear of snakes, believed to be instinctual and rational, is ever-present, and the mere mention of the word 'snake' sends me into a tizzy. I concede it is nature's creature, but one endowed with poisonous fangs.

I pumped him for more details while keeping a nervous eye on the snake's present habitat. What if it crept out unnoticed? 'It can't,' he said. 'The pond has a leak and the water level never rises above the halfway mark.' I wasn't convinced. Surely it can crawl up the side and slide out? 'It tried,' he guffawed with misplaced humour, 'but didn't succeed.' 'What!!!' I grew more jittery.

Word got around. The lady who delivers milk and the odd jobs man filled me in on stories of snakes in the neighbourhood–snakes spotted on cemented yards, snakes dropped by kites on balconies of high rise buildings, snakes wound around trees the scent of whose flowers is believed to repel them, snakes sleeping peacefully over crushed garlic .... It looked as though the creatures were able to surmount all obstacles and were present everywhere. I also heard the shocking story of a victim of snake-bite not being given anti venom for he hadn't brought the snake along. Well, really!

'Do you know there's a snake in our pond?' I said dramatically to my son's friends when they came home two days later and was gratified when Ajay, all of 6 feet and 4 inches, jumped, almost hit the ceiling, and descended on the settee in a heap.

'Krait,' said my husband, announcing the make of his new pet with pride. A former student, who had recently secured top grades for course work on poisonous snakes, and had come by the previous day, had made this alarming identification. Ajay turned pale and immediately pulled his long legs up on the settee, almost folding them into three. I had no idea his ophidiophobia was so acute. 'Why didn't you kill it?' he whispered. My husband replied that it couldn't survive long in the pond anyway, so he had let it be.

That argument didn't befit a conservationist and Ajay took advantage of it. 'How can you think of letting it die a slow, painful death? Call Vava Suresh,' he said urgently. 'I have his number.' Vava Suresh was the admirable young snake catcher whose brave exploits were the toast of the town. 'He never kills snakes. He'll take this one away.'

Vava Suresh was called. He said, 'I'm coming.' 'And I'm going,' said Ajay. He took two huge strides and was out of the house in a flash. Jayaram, the other friend, stayed, ready to film the capture on his mobile. The stage was set and the excitement was palpable. Vava Suresh arrived and from the safety of the window I waited for the drama to unfold. I saw my husband talk to him, probably informing him that it was a krait, quite big and poisonous, and to be careful.

Vava Suresh walked briskly to the pond and in a lightning quick movement, fished it out before Jayaram could even hold the mobile up. 'Eh, this is just a harmless little rat snake,' he commented offhandedly, as he gently caressed its head. 'Give me a plastic bag.' Jayaram took a picture of the snake looking like a worm inside the plastic cover. As Vava Suresh took it away, he said there were two 'serious cases' waiting for him—cobras and vipers.

That was it, a huge anticlimax, over in a jiffy. 'Krait indeed,' I commented, though secretly I was relieved. I think grade inflation has reached new heights.

Coconut Shy

THE BELL RANG AND I OPENED THE DOOR TO FIND A YOUNG man on the doorstep, brandishing a coconut in his right hand like a shot-put athlete getting ready for the throw. 'A coconut,' he said, by way of introduction.

'Oh, a coconut,' I replied.

'Yes, a coconut,' he repeated, pointing to it with his left hand. Now that the identity of the coconut had been established beyond doubt, he continued, 'Yours.'

'Mine?'

'Yes, from your tree.'

'Thanks,' I smiled, holding out my hand.

'No, no,' he cradled the coconut, looking displeased. 'It fell on my auto. Come, take a look.'

Oops, this appeared serious. A student had dropped in a little while before, and both of us meekly followed him to the gate. The auto was parked at a distance and sported a small dent on its mudguard. The sight of the auto loosened the driver's tongue and he turned into a voluble votary of the safety of road users. 'Do you know that a few school children had just passed by? What if it had fallen on them? Look at that old man there. He could have died.' The poor old man, hobbling gamely in the distance, had no idea the possibility of his extinction by an unusual method was being discussed behind his back.

'Or a cyclist,' he continued. 'Yes, it could well have fallen on a cyclist. Or a scooter, a bike, a car...'

What about a bus, a van, a lorry? I wanted to ask. They would object to being left out, if they only knew.

'Why, it could have fallen through the roof of my own auto and landed on my head! Thump! Finished. I had a hair's breadth escape.' The thought sobered him and he looked ghoulishly at us.

I got a little jittery. Should I inform my husband? 'How can you allow such coconuts to be on the tree?' he continued, shaking the coconut like a baby's rattle. What did he want me to do, climb the tree and hold them up? There was no point telling him coconut pickers were hard to come by. My student asked for his number and said we'd get back to him when my husband returned. 'No,' the driver shook his head and the coconut. 'I've come from the outskirts of the city. I don't belong here.'

'So what do you want?' I asked. I was prepared to give him some money for the damage to his vehicle. But instead of coming to the point he began to warm up to his theme, holding forth on the dangers of such coconut trees and soon broadened his subject to include other hazards on the road. I realised he had missed his true vocation; he should have become a teacher, a preacher or a politician.

Carried away by his eloquence, he overplayed his hand. He pointed to the mountain of gravel heaped against my compound wall and said dramatically, 'Look at all that gravel lining the road, leaving no space on the roadside. That forced me to park my auto under the coconut tree.'

Aha, so it was the PWD that was responsible, not me. He had a point. It had been more than a month since the gravel took up residence there, making walking on the road an uphill task. Passing vehicles had been doing a civic service by spreading it all over the place. Now only the tarring required to be done...

Quick to seize my advantage, I was about to relinquish responsibility for the accident when several things happened at once. A few more students turned up, boys, this time. The odd jobs man who happened to be working nearby heard the commotion and came to investigate. A concerned neighbour, who had been watching, shouted from his window upstairs and soon joined us.

From an audience of two nervous women, the auto driver found, the gathering had multiplied unexpectedly. He resumed his speech, but the belligerent new recruits were not mesmerised by his oratory. In fact, they weren't even listening to him. He was discomfited by his sudden vulnerability and decided to leave while the going was good. Turning to go, he mumbled, 'Er, you'd better do something about all these,' and made a sweeping gesture that included the tree, the gravel, the road and everything on it. He handed the coconut to the boy leading the group. 'A coconut', he explained, and disappeared from the scene.

Orchids are Forever

A STUDENT MENTIONED THAT EVERY TIME SHE GOES PAST MY house, she admires the orchids. 'Orchids? You must be kidding,' I replied. 'You've been admiring some other house's garden.' Mine has only a singular orchid, or rather, an orchid in the singular, not a wealth of orchids. I'm no gardener, and the only orchid lending grace to my weedy garden is a gift that had left me perplexed when I received it. The lady who did the honours held the flowerpot at an angle with her delicate, manicured fingers. Believing she didn't wish to soil her hands, I promptly straightened the pot when I got it.

A dainty, elderly lady who was nearby frowned on seeing this and exclaimed, 'Hang it!' I looked at her, surprised. What language in one so dignified! Thankfully the lady who had handed the flowerpot came to my rescue and clarified, 'She means you've got to hang the plant somewhere. It's an orchid and has to be suspended at this angle.'

'Oh, thanks!' I beamed. Orchid! I was elated. It figured high on my list of exotic plants, more to be admired from a distance than possessed, never mind that I couldn't identify one. 'What else?' I asked. Having already exposed my ignorance, I decided to go the whole hog.

'Don't overdo the watering,' I was advised. 'Just pour some water over it once or twice a week.' My heart warmed towards the orchid. How thoughtful and concerned about the time crunch of its caretakers! I love plants that aren't demanding. 'And once in a while,' the helpful orchid expert continued, 'sprinkle it with coconut water or rice gruel.' That's it? So simple. No fancy manure here. And I had believed orchids were high-maintenance. What a plant! I beamed at her again.

Armed with the angled pot and my freshly acquired knowledge, I returned home to scout for the right place to hang it. From the terrace? Not possible. From the wall? Not advisable. Where then? A close examination of my garden yielded no result. I had no idea my front yard was so hanging-pot-unfriendly. I widened my search to include prospective trees whose branches could serve the purpose. Vetoing the coconut trees, the sapota and the olive tree as impractical, I finally zeroed in on the branches of the bilimbi (pulinjaka) tree and fastened the pot securely on a suitable branch.

There it flourishes, hidden among the branches, the flowerpot bent at an angle of 45 degrees, the bright green leaves drooping sensuously to one side, and I swish water over it with a hose whenever I remember. I adore that orchid, it's always got a bunch of mauve blossoms at the end of its long stem. Someone who chanced to glimpse it identified it as a Vanda orchid. Apt name, in fact, 'vandarful'. Eagle-eyed friends vandar why I have punished such a lovely plant, why I allow it to blush unseen. To them I say it blushes only because it is unseen. Else it would have disappeared, like my rose plant.

The few flowerpots standing on a cemented curve near the gate include an anthurium that has willy-nilly survived and a few sad looking rose plants. Rose plants have never flourished in my garden but I always have a few sorry specimens. When I noticed one actually looking healthy, I bestowed all my energies on it, tending it with great care, nurturing it, pruning it and nourishing it with tea dust water and crushed eggshells. I even went after a cow on the road to collect some dung to use as manure.

Just when a few buds began to appear, the plant vanished and in its place I found a pot of weeds. I had rejoiced over the buds that very morning, so who could have spirited it away during the day? Had it changed magically into weeds? The five minutes of a horror movie I had suffered the previous day began to influence my thoughts.

Impatiently, I waited for my husband to return from work to pour out my woes.

'Gone!' I said dramatically. 'Stolen! And in broad daylight!' His eyes went instantly to his scooter. Reassured to see it still standing, he asked for details. I launched into my theory of how the theft could've taken place. '...Someone with a weird sense of humour has stolen it,' I ended my breathless narration after a while.

'It broke,' he confessed sheepishly. 'The hose pulled it down while I was washing the car. The space looked empty, so I placed that pot of weeds there.'

I began my search and after some focussed hunting I finally discovered the rose plant nestling among the shrubs. I rescued it and decided to hang it near the orchid. Safe place, unless the coconut picker has an unerring aim...

SHOPPING WOES

Skin Deep

THE GOLDEN RULE WHEN YOU STEP INTO A SHOP, ESPECIALLY one that sells cosmetics, is to know exactly what you want. The modus operandi, then, is simple. You ask for the item, give it a quick once-over, pay the bill, grab the packet and get the hell out of the place. Hesitate a little, and you are done for.

The other day I entered such a store to buy a hair clip, or maybe hairbands, I wasn't too sure what to get. That irresolution proved to be my undoing. Instead of showing me an array of hair accessories, the smart and well-turned-out attendant turned all her attention to my hair, scrutinising it with such intensity that I began to feel nervous. Whatever was wrong with it? I was sure I didn't have dandruff, my hair was clean, well combed and secured with a hair clip. Maybe the ride in the auto had ruffled it?

I was beginning to think she was speech-impaired when to my relief she broke her silence. The relief was short lived, though, for she began with, 'Why don't you straighten your hair?' I shook my head emphatically. 'No way. My husband calls such hair electrified hair and I don't wish to shock him.' She quickly assured me she hadn't meant permanent straightening. 'We have an excellent hair straightening shampoo. Good for curly hair.' 'No thanks,' I said, 'and my hair is wavy, not curly.' I like to get these things straight.

She scanned my hair again and now that she had found her tongue, there was no stopping her. She aired her views and suggestions freely. My hair looked dull and lifeless. She had just the right shampoo and conditioner for it. Besides, hair should be more vibrant. Had I considered streaks in different colours, just for a change? 'Streak?' I shrieked, my face turning different colours in horror. 'At my age?' She frowned in disapproval at my lack of sportsmanship and reverted to recommending the special shampoo and conditioner. A free hairbrush came with it, she added, a cunning gleam in her eye. 'Free?' I brightened, bit the bait and said, 'I'll take it, I mean, them.'

It was lunchtime and I was the only customer. The other sales girl who had been watching from a distance now came over to join forces with the first attendant. She examined my face minutely, making me blush, and proclaimed, 'All wrong.'

'I know,' I sniffed. 'A poor thing, but my own.' 'I meant your eyebrows,' she said. Ah, I should have seen it coming; I've heard this so often. 'Why don't you shape them?' Pat came my stock reply, 'My husband doesn't approve.'

The first attendant raised her immaculately shaped eyebrows sardonically, as if to say, 'The husband again!' But it was true and like others who had asked me the same question and received the same answer, she declined to comment. A woman can often get away with things by citing her husband's disapproval, but it doesn't work the other way around. If a man were to mumble, 'My wife doesn't like it,' he's bound to invite pitying looks and remarks like, 'Of course, you poor fish, we always knew you were henpecked.'

The second girl peered into my eyes. What she saw pleased her. She informed me jubilantly that three or four of my eyelashes had turned white; she had the perfect mascara to mask it. 'That's all right,' I assured her. 'All of Boris Becker's lashes are blonde.' For the first time she looked uncertain and I pepped up. I had served an ace and I pressed home my advantage. No mascara for me, or any other eye makeup.

She shrugged and curled her red lips into a pout. I was about to ask for my bill when a third attendant, full of good food, strode into the store and promptly joined the Board of Examiners. 'Beginning to sag,' she announced, passing a quick eye over me. 'Eh?' I was shocked. What cheek! 'Your cheeks, jowl, jaw line,' she explained. 'Oh. So?' I retorted. 'Will get worse with neglect,' asserted the first attendant. 'As will the lines on your forehead, around your mouth, your eyes,' the second girl added ominously. 'We have skin tightening creamsssssss,' the third one hissed.

I buckled under this verbal assault and battery. When I left the place, it was with a light purse, a heavy heart and a heavier carry bag. On reaching home I realised I hadn't purchased the hairbands. Or was it a hair clip?

Nothing is Free

WHEN THE BEATLES SANG, 'THE BEST THINGS IN LIFE ARE free...,' they certainly didn't have freebies in mind. But few can resist the lure of something offered for free. I heard my husband tell someone I'd buy a fridge if a pin were offered as a freebie. 'Gross exaggeration!' I denied the charge, then added, 'But for a pen, maybe.' If the pen is mightier than the sword, then a free pen is not to be sneezed at, I'd reckon.

It's the same with bargain offers. Not the best things in life at all, but when a pamphlet arrives, peeping enticingly out of the daily newspaper, informing you in ungrammatical English that's aiming hard to be French—'Speciale Salle! Gete many good's is free'—about a bargain sale, you grab your purse and sail out, all set to jostle your way through suffocatingly overcrowded halls, breathing the oxygen of special offers, elated at the prospect of getting more than your money's worth.

A friend once described his experience of falling into the bargain offer trap. He had gone to a sale where he was offered five pairs of trousers for the price of two and he jumped at it. A pair of trousers gained is a pair of trousers saved and three for free could keep his wife quiet for a few years—an unparalleled bargain. She had been after him to buy a new pair and he was thrilled at the thought of dangling not one but five before her wondering eyes.

Things got lively once he returned home with a carry bag bulging with trousers shoved higgledy-piggledy into it, a leg or two looping out. The zip of the first pair got stuck. When home remedies including using wax on it failed, he gave an almighty tug that ripped the zip right off. The second pair was two sizes too small and though he somehow managed to wriggle in, it took the efforts of the whole family to yank him out of it.

The third went into the washing machine by accident and emerged in a new avatar, changed in colour, texture and size, dyeing his best white shirt and his wife's favourite mauve saree a shocking magenta in the process. The fourth appeared a reasonable fit until he sat down at a meeting. An embarrassing rending sound that drew all eyes to him signalled a tear that ensured he stayed stuck to his seat till everybody left. He gave away the fifth, he said, to the first person who came to him with a hard luck story.

My house is cluttered with useless things either got free or bought at bargain sales. I have a stack of unidentifiable stuff made of plastic that sets my husband's teeth on edge, bedsheets that nervously disintegrate at the sight of water, cracked plates, glasses that break on a whim, a water watch, whatever that means, non-stick pans with remnants of dosa sticking like glue to them, pens that refuse to write and electronic gadgets that had started with a bang and ended immediately with a crackle, pop, fizzle and a final whimper.

True, there's no such thing as a free lunch but I still fall for clever and psychologically astute advertising gimmicks by manufacturers and management gurus. Against my better judgement I go for the attractively packaged junk food only because it brings something free with it, never mind that it is more junk food. Messages on my mobile phone about bargains and exciting promotional offers make me glow with anticipation. Two kilos of rice for the price of one? Here I come! A new coffee brand with a mug free? That's the one for me! A chocolate box with a packet of biscuits is my choice, for sure!

I hate biscuits, the mug is a foul colour and I'm off coffee and chocolates, but what the heck, these things are FREE!!! The freebie might well be substandard stuff or its cost might be included in the price of the main item, but the joy of getting something at no apparent cost gets the better of commonsensical considerations.

The story about the man who bought a packet of oats and returned to the shop to claim the promised free cholesterol might not be far-fetched. Whether it is 'sugar free' or 'cholesterol free,' the operative word—free—influences the choice of brand.

The Beatles knew what marketing was all about when they sang, 'The best things in life are free/ But you can keep them for the birds and bees/ Now give me money/ That's what I want...'

Atishoo, Atishoo!

'ATISHOO, ATISHOO!' I SNEEZED. 'TISSUE, TISSUE!' I HEARD A distorted echo and two boxes of tissues landed on my lap with a plop. A hand thrust a third box under my twitching nose the moment my auto jerked to an annoyed halt after a failed attempt to beat the traffic lights. It was a street vendor taking advantage of these moments of compulsory traffic stoppage to do some quick business at the traffic lights junction. His enterprising family was around, trying to sell various items.

The box under my nose set me off again, making the man drop it. Two sneezes later, I heard him say, 'Three big boxes, only a hundred rupees. Please take, Madam. Very cheap, very useful.' I sniffed into my hanky. I'm a great believer in the good old handkerchief for wiping everything from snot to blood, soil, tears and sweat.

The paper tissue is the rage now, having edged out the faithful handkerchief with clever advertisements that touted the disposable napkin's superior hygiene quotient. As far as historical evidence suggests, the kerchief originated in China in 1000 BCE when the Zhou dynasty had its long innings. It was then used mostly to protect the head, but its fame spread and its potential for other uses made it a popular sartorial embellishment for the rich in Europe. Ladies flaunted their kerchiefs, made of exquisite material, in ancient Rome where games and races began at the drop of a lady's delicate kerchief.

Originally known as kerchief, the word 'hand' was prefixed to it in the 16th century when people began using it to wipe their faces. It worked its way into dowry lists and sometimes led to tragedy, as evidenced by the famous story of Othello whose suspicion that his innocent wife was up to some hanky-panky when he discovered her handkerchief in another man's possession led to deaths all around.

Handkerchiefs served as good luck charms, fashion accessories, status symbols, mementoes, gifts (though in some parts of India there is a superstition that giving hankies as gifts severs the relationship; therefore a token amount of money should exchange hands too) and for advertising during election campaigns.

Who would believe a small piece of embroidered cloth can speak a language? Ask ingenious lovers who used the handkerchief to add a punch to their flirtatious moves. Interestingly, Queen Elizabeth I invented her own handkerchief language by creating a whole vocabulary of kerchief gestures to communicate in silent eloquence with her staff. Another brilliant innovation was during the World Wars. Aviators wore handkerchiefs around their necks that carried maps of the areas they were bombing; so if they were shot down, they had the escape route on their persons.

And then came the disposable paper tissue in the 1930s. Its telling slogan, 'Don't carry a cold in your pocket,' did the trick. Health-conscious people promptly dropped the hanky from their hands and their shopping lists. But now, with scientists of various hues stating that the kerchief is a healthier and an ecologically friendlier alternative to the disposable paper tissue, things look brighter for the handkerchief.

'I don't want these,' I protested. 'Bye.'

'Buy, Madam, buy,' the man implored. I gave up and said, 'I'll take one.' But I had no change. Holding two boxes in one hand and waving a hundred rupee note with the other, I was about to request him to give me the remainder when the lights changed and the auto driver took off with a flourish.

'Tissue!' The man cried and ran across, paying scant attention to the vehicles now on the move. I heard the mad screeching of brakes as the man gave chase to my auto. 'Stop!' I said to the driver who snapped, 'Are you crazy?'

The man, cheered by his family from the other side, sprinted like Usain Bolt and managed to come abreast of the auto which slowed down marginally. I still had the two boxes in one hand and the hundred rupee note in the other. He neatly plucked the hundred out of my fingers, but my protests for change were drowned in the impatient honking of a big fat SUV right behind that forced my auto driver to accelerate.

On reaching home, I again hunted for change; then looked at the pile of tissue boxes. Reading my mind, the driver said, 'paper cash, not paper tissues. And I have change.' I paid him and spotting my environment-conscious husband open the door, left the boxes on the seat of the auto. 'You can take the paper tissues too,' I said and went in.

WHOSE WORD IS IT ANYWAY?

Serving Great Britain

MY HUSBAND SENT ME A MYSTERIOUS TEXT MESSAGE THE other day—'Prabha served a Great Britain for lunch.' I was not in the city and he had been invited to lunch at my friend Prabha's place. But what was she doing, serving Great Britain? I thought we Indians were done with serving the British since August 15 1947. Had an Englishman been invited for lunch too, and like a good Indian, had she served the foreign guest first? And in her enthusiasm to serve him, had she forgotten to serve my husband? No, that couldn't have happened, I reassured myself. Prabha was too perfect a hostess to overlook any of her guests. Or had she served a proper English lunch? She was a great cook and might have gone continental.

I couldn't get this cryptic message out of my mind and sent him a text—'What do you mean?'

I got a reply, 'What do you mean, "what do you mean"?' This was getting us nowhere, not to Great Britain, anyway. So I decided to give him a call to solve the mystery. He was at a meeting and answered in a hoarse whisper, 'I meant she served a great biryani. Don't call again; the meeting's started.'

Ah, so the culprit was the super intelligent autocorrect that knows what's best for everybody and had decided to change the menu to 'Great Britain.' I should have guessed. Don't autocorrect and its older companion spell check delight in making fools of us all?

I remember the joy with which spell check was greeted when it made its confident appearance in our virtual lives. The bumbling spellers were elated and welcomed the programme with fumbling, over-eager fingers. No longer need they misspell 'misspell' or be embarrassed about getting 'embarrassed' wrong. Tricky words could be used fearlessly now, just leave it to Daddy Spell Check.

The idea of crafting a nonsensical sentence like, 'The occurrence of "sacrilegious" in writing was no longer a weird occasion for desperation; instead, the fascinating appellation made you more accommodating and ecstatic,' packed with words that would find a place in Spelling Bee contests, was not daunting anymore.

Competent spellers who cringed when accidental errors crept into their writing were happy too, relieved that with spell check's help, such slips would be corrected automatically and their work would be pristine, pure and mistake-free.

Alas! Little did they guess that spell check worked in unfathomable ways its blunders to perform. As it merrily went about its business, the mechanical, often senseless revision brought with it hilarity, embarrassment and chaos. When a friend tried to use his cousin's name, 'Mrinal', in a mail, spell check claimed to know better and insisted it had better be 'urinal'. An 'erratic schedule' was excitingly altered to an 'erotic schedule' and a happy marriage ran into rough weather when a woman's birthday wishes for her 'dear' husband became ghoulish wishes for her 'dead' husband. Of course, the number of risqué recommendations as substitutes for harmless words and Indian names that the American app struggled to comprehend were countless.

Then came the smartphone with its autocorrect working overtime. The spell check in the computer at least gave the user the option of mulling over the change and overturning its tongue-in-cheek suggestions, but the smartphone with its touch screen mechanism didn't allow any leeway. It was touch and go here—just a light, even accidental touch and the message was gone. A dance recital became rectal, a congratulatory message on someone's happy running of a business changed ominously to happy ruining of a business and parents who were expecting to be asked to take their children for auditioning were appalled to find a message ordering them to be brought for auctioning.

'We're coming to ignite you for our daughter's wedding,' ran a friend's message and we were taken aback. What had we done to this nice friend to have kindled in her a desire for our public immolation? But of course, it was only autocorrect's incendiary substitution for 'invite'.

I sent a message to my husband, 'The stupid autocorrect changed "a great biryani" to "Great Britain". How's the meeting?' I got this text as a response from his smartphone: 'Gored to death here. Dreaming of Great Britain.'

Bored Games

WHEN RAINS FORCE YOU TO STAY INDOORS FOR LONG HOURS, you resort to board games, or are they bored games? No game tries your patience like Scrabble. There is chess, of course, but the great advantage with chess is that you have only one opponent. So if they take ages to make a move, or ask you after sitting motionless for an hour, 'Whose move is it?' you might want to biff them on the head, but nothing worse.

While your opponent gazes intently into the chess board for another hour, drinking it in square by square, you recapitulate your planned moves and take refuge in your own mind. That's what Einstein did when someone asked him at a dull academic meeting if he wasn't terribly bored. 'Oh, no,' Einstein is said to have replied cheerfully, 'on occasions like this, I retire to the back of my mind and there I am happy.'

But in Scrabble you have to reckon with more than one opponent, each with their special quirk. I am yet to find a quiet, quick player who is satisfied with the tiles they have drawn. Once everyone has taken the tiles and examined them, the murmurs of annoyance and dissatisfaction begin. Keep an alert eye for a player who might think an exchange of tiles from the bag on the sly is well within the rules of the game.

There are those who agonise over their tiles and take ages to arrange them on their racks. They hide them like little children, and then make loud remarks that give their letters away: 'Why do I pick only vowels? I can't make "oooieau", can I?'

When you say they certainly can't, loud protests follow. 'But why not? It tells you exactly how I feel now. Check the dictionary. Just let me make that word and get the bonus 50 points for playing a bingo (using all seven tiles at one go) and watch me go "Ouoeaia!"'

There are players who want to get the double or triple word score with x, z or q on the double letter square. There are some others who will not make a good, high-scoring word only because they are opening up the double/triple word space for their opponents. There are also the kind who use their turn to discard all their tiles, only to pick up another set of vowels, setting them grumbling forever. Even when players manage to score a bingo, they feel distressed they didn't have letters of greater value or that they hadn't got a triple or at least a double word score.

One rainy day a cousin turned up and suggested we play a game of Scrabble. The board was missing. Someone remembered it had been in the cupboard attacked by the termites. Had they got at it? I couldn't recall conducting the last rites for a half-eaten board. They wouldn't have eaten the tiles anyway, they were plastic. We finally found the frayed board lying hidden under the Snakes and Ladders in the steel almirah. We discovered the tiles in a rusty chocolate tin marked 'Nails', as also three racks and three small scoreboards. We picked these out carefully and transferring the tiles to a cloth pouch, began the game.

After half an hour of brooding and sighing, the cousin came up with 'toil'. My husband confessed he had only consonants and took another half an hour to take advantage of the vowels used by the cousin to make the three-letter word, 'tot'.

'I didn't want to make a four letter word with three letters,' he said virtuously. 'Or can I?'

Disputes erupted. What's wrong with four letter words? They are all in the dictionary. What about hyphenated words and exclamations, then? They are also in the dictionary.

After two hours that interspersed arguments with long silences, the cousin exclaimed, 'Bingo!' and placed six blanks and an E on the board. 'The word's "illegal",' he explained.

'Six blanks? Impossible,' I protested. 'There are only two blanks per set. This is illegal.' We had made our own rule of replacing used blanks on the board with the relevant letters when we drew them and didn't realise this was happening too often.

We found more blank tiles. The mystery was solved when we discovered bits of cello tape stuck to the inner sides of the tin and remembered we had fixed the tape on the tiles so that the letters wouldn't fade. But they had gone a step further and come away with the tape.

We jettisoned Scrabble and took up Monopoly.

The She I Love

'MY MEMORY, MY MEMORY!' I MOANED, PEERING INTO THE cupboard.

'Why, do you think it could be lying hidden inside?' my husband wisecracked.

'Funny!' I replied, wondering for the nth time why I had opened the cupboard in the first place. To get something from it, no doubt, but what that something was, I just couldn't recall.

I don't know about you, but this happens very frequently to me. I spend so much time in front of the open fridge, kitchen cupboards, almirahs, book shelves and drawers trying to remember what I'd come for, that I'm sure if I timed myself, I would be a prime contender for the Guinness Maximum Time Spent In Front Of Cupboards Wondering Why You Were Standing There Scratching Your Head record.

'Don't know what you came looking for?' This time my husband's guess was correct. 'Haha, not to worry, happens to everybody. And to a chosen few, more than others,' he added, rummaging through the adjacent cupboard. He moved away and sauntered to the door with a cheerful, 'Bye!'

'Where are you going?' I asked.

'I have a class today. Forgotten that too?' He grinned. 'You're getting good at this.'

'And you're getting better. You've forgotten your shirt.' It was my turn to grin. I looked at him—all set to go for his class, a brilliant lecture in his head but no shirt on his person—and stopped worrying about my memory playing hide-and-seek.

That evening something happened that was even more reassuring. A friend sent the link to an old Mohammed Rafi song, *The She I Love*, a rare one that he had sung in English to the tune of a popular Hindi number. Believe it or not, the moment I saw the title, every single word of the song came back to my mind as if it had been imprinted on my memory. And I had not even sung it all these years! I began to hum, 'The She I love is a beautiful, beautiful dream come true...,' mentally giving my memory appreciative pats on its back.

But the tune got stuck in my head and soon began to irritate me. I remembered my husband mentioning a word to describe a song or a tune that keeps repeating in one's mind. My memory let me down again for I couldn't remember the word, but I knew there was a worm in it. The moment he returned from his class, wondering what was for tea, I asked, 'It's earthworm, isn't it?'

'For tea?' He looked appalled.

'No, no, the word that means having a song in your ear that keeps playing continuously. I thought you said it was some worm. Earthworm?'

'Earthworm? How can an earthworm be in your ear? Use your common sense.' His hunger made him brusque. I protested it wasn't impossible to have an earthworm in your ear. 'It could always be put there,' I said, for the sake of argument. 'Not the nicest of prospects, but definitely possible.' He didn't give ear to my words and continued from where he had left off. 'It's called "earworm",' he said, heading for the dining table.

Ah, earworm, that's it. While he had his tea, I found out more about the unattractive word. It was a very old word in English, but had been used to refer to the earwig that was erroneously believed to get into people's ears. In most languages, that is what the 'earworm' had stood for until it began to be used to allude to a pest that infected ears of corn.

In the 1960s, the Germans, with typical German acumen, applied the word 'ohrwurm', meaning 'earworm', to describe any irritating or catchy piece of music that burrowed into your head and got fixed there. The English found the expression appropriate and appropriated its literal translation for the purpose so that, in the 1980s, the re-invented 'earworm' wiggled its way into the English language.

Pleased with my new knowledge, I reported my findings to my husband and followed that with the reason for my sudden interest in the word. 'It all started with *The She I Love*, my new earworm.' And just to prove I remembered it verbatim, I sang the whole song, totally off-key, to him.

'That song is plaguing me now,' he grumbled at dinner, glaring at the she he loved, as if she was a nightmare. I was standing near the open fridge, wondering what I wanted from it. 'Beat it!' I exclaimed, singing my latest earworm, and took an egg out.

Aunty or Madam

'WHAT A LOVELY SAREE!' I EXCLAIMED WHEN I SIGHTED my friend. I don't know how many men receive compliments when they wear nice shirts but when a woman wears a pretty saree, it is imperative to praise her impeccable taste. 'Thanks! But, ah!' she gave a wistful sigh. 'You should have seen the one I did not buy, the one that got away.'

'Got away? Why? How?' I sensed an interesting story here.

Now her tone changed dramatically from wistful to belligerent. 'That salesman, old enough to be my grandfather, rather, father, er, at least my older brother, actually called me "aunty". Imagine! What nonsense!' She looked outraged as she continued her tirade. 'How dare he? Tell me, do I look old enough to be his aunty? Or, for that matter, anyone's aunty?'

Not having seen the salesman, I couldn't offer an opinion regarding the first of her indignant questions, so I made a few relevant noises. But I responded to her second question with a diplomatic silence. Having first become an aunt at eight, I believe there is no particular age for attaining aunthood. But wait a minute, she wasn't talking about age; it was all about looks.

I gave her a surreptitious once-over and the silence continued to be diplomatic until I broke it to ask, 'So where did you buy this beautiful saree?'

She brightened. 'Oh, at another showroom. Such a sweet salesman there. So frank and forthright too. He said, "Madam, this saree will suit your fair complexion."'

So that was the secret formula. A little less of 'aunty-ing' and a little more of 'madam-ing' with a bit of flattery on the side would have helped up the sales of that unsuspecting, honest salesman who had provoked my friend to leave his shop in high dudgeon. Business establishments that wish to flourish would do well to invest in a 'madam-ing' and 'sir-ing' skills training programme for their staff.

The older a woman gets, the more she takes umbrage at unflattering modes of address. How ironic, I thought, that the same girls who, while in college demanded that their juniors, if only by a day, showed respect by calling them 'Chechi'(meaning 'older sister' in Malayalam), wished to be called either by their names or by the diplomatic honorific, 'Madam' when they grew older, but not wiser.

This 'Chechi' business hadn't been in practice when I was a student for I remember how we addressed all our seniors by their names, and there was no dearth of respect shown either, especially towards those who were bossy or burly.

What does it matter, anyway, I told myself rather self-righteously, whether you are addressed as aunty, madam or chechi? Who cares about such petty things?

But, of course, I had underestimated my own vanity.

A few days later, I was at a bakery, buying some snacks, and the bill came to sixty-one rupees. Observing me draw out a hundred rupee note from my purse, the owner began to fumble around in his cash box. Peering in, I spotted a fifty-rupee note nestling in it. I thought I could help him out by giving him an extra eleven rupees so that he could give me the fifty. Handing him the hundred, I began to rummage in my purse for the change when he looked up and asked, 'Amma, do you have eleven rupees? Then I can give you a fifty rupee note.'

I froze. Amma? Whose amma? What amma? When amma? Wherefore amma? This grey-haired great-grandfather with a dome for a forehead had been running this bakery since the time I was in school, when I was in short skirts and had my hair in two plaits. He had been around for donkey's years, might have hit a century even. Who was he calling 'amma'? I closed my purse with a telling click.

'Hunt, hunt,' my thoughts churned indignantly in my head. 'Turn the cash box upside down. Turn out your pockets. Look in the pockets of the long underpants centurions like you must wear. Collect all the loose change and find out if it adds up to thirty-nine. Borrow from your assistant. Go ask at the neighbouring shop. There's a grouch there who doesn't know the meaning of help. Or appeal to the beggar in the corner. Buy some fruit from the fruit seller with the hundred. You might, just might, get the change you require. But don't expect any assistance from me. I'll wait till kingdom come, but no way am I parting with my eleven!'

'Madam, do you have eleven rupees in change?' the canny, middle-aged assistant asked me. I smiled and opened my purse, my good humour restored...

www.ingramcontent.com/pod-product-compliance
Lightning Source LLC
LaVergne TN
LVHW010323070526
838199LV00065B/5641